Three Minutes a Day

VOLUME 44

THREE MINUTES A DAY
VOLUME 44

Rev. Dennis Cleary, M.M.
The Christophers

Mary Ellen Robinson
Vice President, The Christophers

Stephanie Raha
Editor-in-Chief

Margaret O'Connell
Senior Research Editor

Contributors
Joan Bromfield
Monica Ann Yehle Glick
Karen Hazel Radenbaugh
Anna Marie Tripodi

Contributing Interns
Melissa Hayden
Mary Beth Mullarkey
Maria Puig
Jill Wronski

The Christophers
5 Hanover Square, 11th Floor
New York, NY 10004

(Jesus) said..."Do not worry about your life, what you will eat, or about your body, what you will wear. For life is more than food, and the body more than clothing. ...Can any of you by worrying add a single hour to your span of life? If then you are not able to do so small a thing as that, why do your worry about the rest? ...Your Father knows that you need them. Instead, strive for His kingdom, and these things will be given to you as well.

LUKE 12:22-23, 25-26, 30-31

Preface

Warm greetings from The Christophers to each of you! Whether you're an old friend of *Three Minutes a Day* or a first-time reader, you're in for a special treat. This newest edition of one of our perennial favorites is full of stories that will get each day of the year off to an inspiring start.

In the same way, your interest and spirit encourage our work and message. It is especially heartening for us to know that we have friends such as you who appreciate our efforts. The letters coming in from all over the world assure us that our Christopher material and programs make a real difference in peoples' lives. It's our daily reminder that one candle can truly light another!

Because of the special sacrifices made by our "partners" everywhere, new horizons continue to open for all of us. That in turn inspires us to reach out to millions more with our words of hope and encouragement, leading them to the kind of positive and constructive action that will shape the future toward God.

May the year be filled with many blessings for you and yours!

Mary Ellen Robinson
Vice President
The Christophers

Introduction

As we begin the last year of the first decade of this Millennium, I welcome you to this 44th edition of The Christophers' *Three Minutes a Day*.

An unknown author once wrote about life:

"Life is a challenge—meet it

Life is a gift—accept it.

Life is eternal—believe it."

The Christophers' founder, Father James Keller, M.M., knew that to embrace life each person needs to renew the spark that kindles the *interior* life. That's why he wrote the first book of this series. Today, each page still offers an opportunity for renewal.

In these times, work, chores and distractions gobble up every waking moment. Yet, this book only requires three minutes, one hundred and eighty seconds. The stories can inspire you; help you see things differently; even offer wisdom. Take those three minutes to reflect, to refresh yourself, so that over the course of the year, you will quench your thirst for God's life-giving water.

Rev. Dennis Cleary, M.M.
The Christophers

New Year Wishes

As the old year ends and a new one begins, it's only natural to think about the past, and especially, the future.

Here's something First Lady Eleanor Roosevelt wrote in one of her newspaper columns during the Great Depression: "I wish for those I love this New Year an opportunity to earn sufficient; to have that which they need for their own and to give that which they desire to others; to bring into the lives of those about them some measure of joy; to know the satisfaction of work well done, of recreation earned and therefore savored; to end the year a little wiser, a little kinder and therefore a little happier."

May each of us use the turn of the New Year to resolve to try each day to seek and strive for our own true welfare and the welfare of others.

Why do you see the speck in your neighbor's eye, but do not notice the log in your own eye? (Luke 6:41)

Bless us, Father of all, as another year begins.

Defying the Odds — As Usual

Dustin Carter doesn't consider himself unusual. The high-school wrestler's legs end at the knee; his right arm stops just at the elbow and his left is even shorter. Yet he has a wrestling record of 41 wins and 2 losses and has won several tournaments. But that doesn't strike Carter, from Goshen, Ohio, as any reason to be thought special. "I wrestle like anybody else," he says.

Carter, who had his limbs amputated after contracting a serious infection when he was five, says he gets by just fine. In fact, his athletic accomplishments seem to take a second place to his perseverance. While nearly every task poses a challenge, Carter makes it look easy. He unscrews drinking water bottles with his teeth; lifts himself up to reach things; and writes by gripping a pen with both arms.

"I don't like people feeling sorry for me," he says.

Don't feel sorry for someone with disabilities. Admire and emulate their courage.

"Do not fear, greatly beloved, you are safe. Be strong and courageous!" (Daniel 10:19)

May I draw inspiration from disabled people, Eternal God.

Plant a Green Bough

There's a lovely Chinese proverb worth contemplating: "If I keep a green bough in my heart, the singing bird will come." Inspirational writer William Arthur Ward suggests there "are five 'green boughs' we should strive to keep in our hearts:"

1. **Enthusiasm** — "Where there is positive excitement, there is more sparkle in the eye, and zest in the living."

2. **Kindness** — "Kindness is the Golden Rule in action."

3. **Generosity** — "This is the golden key that unlocks the gates of joy, fulfillment and life more abundant."

4. **Humor** — "If we learn to laugh at ourselves we will always be amused."

5. **Gratitude** — "With gratitude in our hearts, there can be no room for self-pity, resentment or bitterness."

Open yourself to the wonders of God's blessings, whatever form they may take.

Out of the abundance of the heart the mouth speaks. (Matthew 12:34)

Your gifts and Your grace are the essence of our lives, Spirit of God. Help us appreciate them.

The Great Big Book of Everything

Harvard biologist E. O. Wilson is on a mission. He's trying to create an electronic "Encyclopedia of Life" (EOL) covering every organism on the planet, from plants and animals to microorganisms. This Internet-based information will include everything known about each species.

It will be an invaluable resource, not only for research but also for practical applications—for example, the farmer whose crops are being eaten by a mysterious beetle or the person worried about a sick Siamese cat.

The real key, Wilson says, is that the EOL will help us to better understand life on Earth. "And we can't save the planet if we don't understand it," he explains.

We are each stewards of God's creation, each called to do our part to preserve the life around us and within us.

Is it lawful to do good or to do harm...to save life or to kill? (Mark 3:4)

Lord of life, guide our efforts to preserve every creature You have fashioned.

Running a Tab — for the Neighborhood

Signs of hard times were everywhere, and Sam saw them among the regulars at his small cafe. In one week, two people had lost their jobs, downsized in a faltering economy.

Feeling the effects of the same financial downturn, Sam couldn't afford to lend others cash, but he could give food to his neighbors.

At closing time one Sunday evening, he offered one man a few items, noting they would spoil before he re-opened mid-week. He also gave a woman an order of food that he said was prepared by mistake. These people had supported his business, and now Sam felt it was his turn to help them.

When times are tough, we can each do our part, no matter how small, to bring a bit of relief to someone in need.

Those who oppress the poor insult their Maker, but those who are kind to the needy honor Him. (Proverbs 14:31)

Blessed Trinity, You know me and what I need. Surround me always with Your love.

Facing—and Conquering—Stress

Stressed? Who isn't, you say. Want to respond to stress in a way that relieves it? Here are some suggestions:

- Say "I don't know" when you genuinely do not know. Inventing an answer to cover your ignorance only causes anxiety.

- In a conversation or argument, listen to the other person's point of view even if you disagree. This shows that you value that person's perspective.

- When doing something outside your comfort zone, focus on the "I can" rather than on the "I can't."

- Know when to say "No." You cannot please everyone all the time. Too, exceeding your personal limits will only add to your anger and stress.

Am I not allowed to do what I choose? (Matthew 20:15)

Holy Spirit, help me know my limits. Inspire my decisions.

When Cyberspace Can and Should Wait

Catherine Madera relished any free time she could get to catch up on e-mails and web surf. A wife, mother, and homemaker, Madera had little time to call her own. She logged on early each day, before her family awoke and the breakfast and off-to-school rush began.

One day, though, her husband Mark suggested she turn off her computer and share morning coffee with him. "I'm working on some stuff," she replied, shrugging off his invitation. But a few days later she realized that she shared very little time with her husband, yet carried on meaningful e-mail communications with friends.

Today, Madera has a new routine. She awakens each day to share morning coffee with her husband. "I love my computer, but not at the expense of my family," she says.

Make more time for your spouse and family.

Just after daybreak, Jesus stood on the beach...they saw a charcoal fire there, with fish on it, and bread...Jesus said to them, "Come and have breakfast." (John 21:4,9,12)

Risen Savior, who prepared breakfast for Your well-loved disciples, remind us to break bread with our loved ones each day.

A Creative Use for Giveaways

You are probably familiar with the toiletry samples many hotels and motels give to guests for their convenience. Small bottles of shampoo, lotion and bars of soap are typical, as are shoe buffers and shower caps.

The Saint Olaf Parish Women's Council in Bountiful, Utah, found a creative and generous use for such items. Each year, the Council holds its Stocking Stuffer and Potluck Dinner, where parishioners gather to fill over 500 stockings with these samples and giveaways they collect while traveling on business or vacation. The filled stockings are delivered to men, women and children in need of everyday personal care items.

Perhaps one of the nicest things about Saint Olaf's tradition is the fact that small children participate in the event, stuffing stockings for the needy.

Children learn by watching others. Set a compassionate example by giving to those in need and by speaking about poor people respectfully.

Clothe yourselves with compassion. (Colossians 3:12)

Help me put my faith into action, God.

Pick Your Own Attitude

It's a matter of attitude.

Whether we tend to see a glass as half empty or as half full, our attitudes color our whole lives. More than that, while how we think about the world and ourselves affects our decisions, our decisions affect our perspective.

As religious writer Charles Swindoll said, "We have a choice everyday regarding the attitude we will embrace for that day. Life is 10 per cent what happens to me and 90 per cent how I react to it. And so it is with you. We are in charge of our attitudes."

Optimism should not deny the reality of pain and problems, but giving in to constant negativity is equally unrealistic. The French magazine *Psychologies* recommends "intelligent optimism" which focuses on things you can change rather than on what you cannot.

You can't change everything, but you can always change something for the better including your way of looking at life.

Hope does not disappoint us, because God's love has been poured into our hearts through the Holy Spirit. (Romans 5:5)

Inspire me to say "Yes!" to Your goodness, Your joy, Your will, Almighty Father.

The Wonders of a Washer and Dryer

Brenda Hopkins has her hands full, literally. She is raising a grandson who has severe attention deficit disorder. And, because of end stage renal failure and high blood pressure, she needs renal dialysis three times a week.

Hopkins had to walk up and down four flights of stairs with bags of laundry three times weekly. Given her serious health problems, this task often left her feeling listless and worn down. Worse, the exertion helped cause her legs to swell, resulting in excruciating pain.

Alerted by Hopkins' social worker, *The New York Times'* Neediest Cases Fund helped the Brooklyn Bureau of Community Service buy her a washer and dryer for her apartment. "It's a huge help," she says, adding that her life has become less stressful in general.

Donations helped make needed household appliances a reality for one woman. What can your donations, pooled with others', do for people in need?

The rich and the poor have this in common: the Lord is the maker of them all. (Proverbs 22:2)

Instill in me the drive to serve others out of the fullness of Your gifts to me, Gracious God.

Healthy Aging

Here are some tips on healthy aging from the centenarians of the Nicoya Peninsula, Costa Rica as reported by Dan Buettner in *AARP Magazine*.

- Have a strong sense of a goal, a clear mission in life
- Focus on your family. Family provides support, purpose and belonging.
- Maintain social networks. Visit. Listen. Laugh. Appreciate what you have.
- Keep hard at work at daily physical chores.
- Embrace your heritage, including spiritual traditions.
- Eat lightly and include a wide variety of vegetables.

Life is God's gift to each one of us. In gratitude and because good health is so valuable, do all you can to live a long, vigorous and useful life.

Jesus said..."I am the bread of life. Whoever comes to Me will never be hungry, and whoever believes in Me will never be thirsty." (John 6:35)

Bless my efforts to live in a health-promoting and enhancing way, Jesus.

Showing Good Taste

If you think your cup of coffee tastes better when served in a nice cup or mug, you're not alone. Aradha Krishna, a marketing professor at the University of Michigan, says, "Rationally the feel of a container should not affect taste." Yet it does.

In a study, 1,000 college students were blindfolded and given water in firm or flimsy cups. The majority rated the taste of the water in flimsy cups far more negatively than that in more substantial cups, although the water was the same in both.

Interestingly, students with a low sensitivity to touch gave the worst evaluations to the flimsy-cup water. Researchers think that people who are more sensitive to touch (e.g., those who tend to touch items frequently when shopping) understand when touch is important, and when not.

It's easy to be affected by outside influences. Let's pay more attention to what really matters when making choices.

Discretion and tongue and eyes, ears and a mind for thinking He gave them. He filled them with knowledge and understanding. (Sirach 17:6-7)

Creator, guide us in seeking the truth in all things.

Positive Thinking, Cold Comfort

We live in a culture in which wearing a "game face," or brave exterior, amidst dire circumstances is considered a virtue.

Take actor Patrick Swayze. Like many celebrities confronted with personal challenges, Swayze, who is battling pancreatic cancer, shows a bright-eyed, confident smile when in public. Likewise, Massachusetts Senator Ted Kennedy, now fighting brain cancer, gave a decisive "thumbs up" to crowds of onlookers when he left the hospital, symbolizing positive thinking and optimism, despite the gravity of his diagnosis.

Some experts say such displays of optimism serve to reassure anxious loved ones, and give hope to those fighting their own tough problems. Others disagree, saying that such behavior reinforces unrealistic expectations, stifles healthy expressions of grief and fear, and belies the individual's true suffering.

Embracing honesty, as well as hope, is the best approach. Says one cancer patient coping with sadness, "Just let me be where I am right now."

Honesty comes home to those who practice it. (Sirach 27:9)

Messiah, bring relief and serenity to the suffering.

The Power of Pets

They aren't called human's best friends for nothing. Recent research indicates that owning a dog or any pet can be beneficial to a person's health. Dr. Steven Garner, who writes a medical column, shares these interesting facts about pet ownership:

- Men with a pet are six times more likely to be alive six months after a heart attack than those without a pet.
- Women aged 50 to 60 recover from breast cancer treatment more quickly if they own a pet.
- Pet owners made 15-20 per cent fewer annual visits to the doctor than non-pet owners.
- Pets reduce stress, and can increase the level of endorphins in the brain.

Says one believer, "My 85-year old father has had a dramatic transformation recently. He adopted a dog, and has a more youthful, positive outlook on life than before."

Companion animals are part of this wonderful world that God created. Love and respect them as such.

It is required of stewards that they be found trustworthy. (1 Corinthians 4:2)

Instill in your people a spirit of compassionate stewardship, Creator.

Second Helpings, Anyone?

It seems that Indianapolis-based non-profit group Second Helpings truly lives up to its moniker. The organization offers free, nutritious meals to low-income people in the Indianapolis area and also opens the door to a second chance at life for many.

Inspired by its mission, "To eliminate hunger and empower people," the 21-member staff of Second Helpings seeks to improve the lives of those in need through job training, food rescue, hunger relief and companionship.

Six days a week, staff members, culinary students and volunteers prepare 2,900 hot and ready-to-eat meals. To do this, the group embarks on food rescue efforts, collecting more than 100,000 pounds of donated perishable and overstocked food every month.

One volunteer says, "It's the happiest place I've ever worked."

There is something liberating about focusing on others' needs. Tap into the joy and serenity that comes through service.

Like good stewards of the manifold grace of God, serve one another with whatever gift each of you has received. (1 Peter 4:10)

Lead me to a life of service, Savior.

Parents Welcome!

Writer Ari Goldman recounts how he, as a New York City parent, accompanied his son Judah to orchestra practice every Tuesday night. "While the 7- to 13-year olds played beautiful music, I, along with all the other parents, would read newspapers, check e-mail and wait until the rehearsal ended," he says.

One evening, Goldman says he "couldn't take it anymore." He didn't want to merely listen to his son's orchestra practice; he wanted to play along with him.

Goldman hadn't played cello in decades, and admits the idea of joining his son's orchestra seemed a bit crazy. Still, he mustered his courage. "There's something about music that cuts across generation," says Goldman, who was welcomed into the orchestra by the conductor.

Although Goldman played with the group for only one season, the experience was exhilarating. "I'd do it again in a heartbeat," he says.

Joy is available to all. What brings you joy?

May the God of hope fill you with all joy and peace. (Romans 15:13)

Inspire my search for joy; encourage me to cultivate what brings me joy, Holy Spirit.

Unreasonable Resumes

Men and women who are out of work probably feel at some point that they would try just about anything to get the attention of a prospective employer. Yet having someone notice you for the wrong reason rarely gets good results.

Here are some ways job-seekers tried to get a new position:

- One person cut up a resume into six puzzle pieces and sent them separately for the employer to assemble.

- Another sent an egg carton with fake eggs and promised to deliver fresh ideas everyday.

- An applicant posted a large sign with his qualifications on a building across the street from the employer.

Unfortunately, a survey by a job search company concluded that most executives view such unusual job-hunting ploys as unprofessional.

Channel your talents and creativity simply and directly.

Commit your work to the Lord. (Proverbs 16:3)

Blessed Trinity, grant me the wisdom to use Your gifts appropriately for myself and others.

The Last Hours of a Leader

On the 40th anniversary of the Rev. Dr. Martin Luther King, Jr.'s assassination in 2008, writers, commentators and historians reflected on the civil rights leader's impact on American history and society.

The personal details of King's last hours are interesting. For example, the men who accompanied King on that fateful evening in Memphis, Tennessee on April 4, 1968, were all young. No surprise, then, that King and his friends had a pillow fight hours before he was shot.

Another source reports that King's final thoughts encompassed gospel music, neckties, soul food and the high price of righteousness. "I'd rather be dead than afraid," the oft-threatened civil rights leader explained to his friends that day.

When assassins killed King, they killed not only a leader but a pastor, a husband and a father.

Engage in non-violent, respectful political disagreement if and when you must. Our ideas may differ, but we are all human.

Jesus said..."Put your sword back...for all who take the sword will perish by the sword." (Matthew 26:52)

Gracious Lord, may we respect each other's opinions.

The Truly Abundant Life

Overdrawn checking. No savings. Maxed out credit cards. Bursting closets. Overstuffed home. Garage too full for the car. Barely current with the mortgage. Yet you still want more. Maybe it's time to cultivate *enough-ness*.

Begin and end your day with gratitude for another day of life, for your family, for the weather, for your home, for God's care, for creatures tame and wild, for Earth's loveliness.

Be open, loving and generous with yourself. Treat yourself to extra time to read, sleep or just vegetate. Enjoy a sunny day out of doors. Make time for others.

Donate or sell what you haven't used in a year or more. Give to those who are in need, including thrift shops, shelters. Ask yourself if a contemplated purchase is a necessity or something meant to impress others.

Above all, remember that how much you really have is your choice.

Life does not consist in the abundance of possessions. (Luke 12:15)

Unclench my grasping hands, Liberator. Show me just how rich I am.

Enough!

In her 20 years as a gynecologist, Dr. Hilda Hutcherson has helped women from all backgrounds: rich, poor, and in between. Despite their diversity, she has found many share a common concern: dissatisfaction with their own bodies.

Dr. Hutcherson attributes this growing dissatisfaction to a society that "dissects women into many little parts, with each part needing to be surgically altered so that you can become the perfect woman."

While much of this message comes from the media: "do this diet...take this medication...to perfect." She asks, "is anybody really perfect?"

What media images offend or disturb you? Do these images show women in a positive way? Consider expressing your views to your local television station and to advertisers who support such programming.

Charm is deceitful, and beauty is vain but a woman who fears the Lord is to be praised. Give her a share in the fruit of her hands, and let her works praise her in the city gates. (Proverbs 31:30-31)

Encourage women and girls to see themselves with Your accepting, loving eyes, Holy Spirit.

Healing Beneath the Palms

Some of the visitors strolling along Antigua's pristine beaches may be there for more than the sun and fun. There's a new drug and alcohol addiction treatment facility there, The Crossroads Centre, which offers a healing environment for recovering addicts.

Funded by rock-music superstar Eric Clapton and guided by Father Frank Power, SVD, the Center helps recovering addicts focus on the underlying causes of their addictions which typically include what Father Power calls "poverty of the soul"— despite their personal wealth.

In their sessions, clients, aided by the tranquil scenery of the Caribbean, begin to consider the positives in their lives, and develop a sense of gratitude, along with self-forgiveness.

Money isn't really everything. Give your time, talent and attention to help nourish someone's soul and your own.

At dinner in Levi's house, many tax collectors and sinners were also sitting with Jesus...the scribes...(asked)..."Why does He eat with tax collectors and sinners?"...He said..."I have come to call not the righteous but sinners." (Mark 2:15,16,17)

Comfort those who are aching for meaning, Lamb of God.

Stepping Off the Hamster Wheel

Maggie's life seemed an endless "to do" list, one that stretched way beyond her demanding job. Then she had to have major surgery.

Suddenly, she had to say "no" to activities and requests that had, in the past, taken her away from her family. Instead, as she recovered, she found herself spending long afternoons just talking with her 10-year-old daughter. They watched hours of their favorite movies and tried new recipes for family dinners. Too there was the time for reconnecting with her husband.

As she prepared to return to work, Maggie decided she liked the new schedule for her hours outside of work. She wouldn't be filling that time up again with any thing other than family and family fun.

Sometimes we need to stop for a moment in order to get our lives moving again in the right direction.

Every matter has its time and way, although the troubles of mortals lie heavy upon them. (Ecclesiastes 8:6)

Time is Your precious gift, Lord. Help us to fill it wisely.

A Little Patch of Green

Some 40 years ago, the Dominican Sisters of St. Mary of the Springs bought 160 acres in Franklin County, Ohio, as a place of tranquility and beauty. They named it Shepherd's Corner.

Since then, urban development, buildings and traffic have encircled what was to have been a quiet rural setting. Rather than leave, the Sisters stood firm. "We're an oasis where people can reconnect with nature," says one of the site's seasonal employees.

Today, Shepherd's Corner, one of the area's last remnants of rural beauty offers retreats and is also a working farm and educational center. "The farm stands as a symbol of what this area used to be, and something the neighbors don't want to lose," says Sister Diane Kozlowski.

Progress is admirable, but too often we lose as much as we gain. What parts of your area should be preserved?

You set the earth on its foundations...cover it with the deep...make springs gush forth...giving drink to every wild animal...birds...sing among the branches...(You) cause the grass to grow for the cattle, and plants for people.
(Psalm 104:5,6,10,11,12,14)

May we respect and honor the Earth, Your creation and our home, Creator.

The Milkman's On His Way — Again

Forty years ago, many people didn't have to dash to the store each day "to pick up some milk." The milk came to their kitchen doorstep via their friendly neighborhood milkman.

The earliest survey on home milk delivery by the Department of Agriculture dates to 1963, when nearly 30 per cent of American consumers had their milk delivered to their doors. By 1975, that percentage dropped to under seven percent.

Today, home milk delivery is making a comeback in some areas. In Wisconsin and Illinois, for example, demand for home delivery has surged. The reasons? Convenience, of course. And, control: deliveries can be suspended, doubled, whatever, at the click of a mouse. Plus, many consumers enjoy patronizing local businesses which has helped reestablish home milk delivery.

Funny how things once thought passé can come back into vogue again. What's next? Doctors' house calls?

What has been is what will be, and what has been done is what will be done; there is nothing new under the sun. (Ecclesiastes 1:9)

Help me weather the changes and seasons of my life, Dear Savior.

Growing Families

The sign above the door reads, "God sets the rainbow in the clouds." For the parents that make their way through that doorway to the Neonatal Intensive Care Unit (NICU) at Einstein Hospital in the Bronx, New York, the saying echoes the hope offered by the staff inside.

"Our unit is all about nurturing, growing and developing the family unit," explains Jeanne DeMarzo, NICU nurse manager.

Most of the tiny patients have been born prematurely, and require advanced medical attention. This means parents must leave the hospital without their newborns.

To make the atmosphere warmer, volunteers painted the wall in the family lounge with a mural of butterflies, trees and flowers. And several NICU nurses regularly knit and crochet small blankets for the little ones in their care.

Whether the difficulties are in our lives, or the lives of others, we should look for a way to help the light shine through the darkness.

Rouse Yourself! Why do You sleep, O Lord? Awake, do not cast us off forever!...Rise up, come to our help. Redeem us for the sake of Your steadfast love. (Psalm 44:23,26)

In my fear and longing, I turn to You, Father. Answer my prayers.

Biking For Change

According to an article in *Catholic Digest,* members of Brake the Cycle of Poverty began as parishioners at a Connecticut church who wanted to help the poor.

Today the teachers, insurance agents, engineers, and others are teammates, cycling through Connecticut to raise awareness of local poverty and injustice. They give presentations, talk to politicians and visit poverty centers.

You may not be able to pedal, but you can still PEDAL:

Participate with a local social justice group.

Educate others with the information at www.povertyusa.

Donate your time, surplus goods, when possible, money.

Advocate by writing to editors, politicians.

Love and respect others.

John Donne reminds us that: "No man is an island" and "I am involved in mankind."

I will draw near...for judgment...against those who oppress the hired workers...the widow and the orphan...who thrust aside the alien...says the Lord. (Malachi 3:5)

Abba, remind us that as Your children we are each other's siblings.

Building Peace

When Cindy Woodruff's mother was diagnosed with breast cancer, Woodruff began thinking about the meaning of her own life. That's when she heard about Jella Lepman who had fled Nazi Germany and, after the war, had been asked to return to help children heal by focusing on kids' imagination through literature.

So Woodruff decided to establish a Peace Study Center to teach conflict resolution and help children talk about feelings in peaceful ways. Kits for teachers include music, DVDs, curriculum guides, notebooks, puppetry and scripts for skits.

Woodruff says, "When you give children language to work with, putting labels to emotions, they're empowered to go places and learn things and be with other people in a peaceful way."

Fear is often an excuse for violence and rudeness. Too, it limits children and adults; organizations and nations. How can you substitute knowledge and respect for ignorance and violence?

Owe no one anything, except to love one another; for the...commandment(s) are summed up in...'Love your neighbor as yourself'. (Romans 13:8,9)

Help me see the innate humanity of all peoples no matter how much they may differ from me, Creator.

Advice to Live By

Lauretta and Ray Seabeck followed the advice of Mother Teresa of Calcutta, "Pray, believe and love, and that will lead to action."

Their own prayers, faith and caring concern, and a written invitation from Mother Teresa herself, led this New Hampshire couple to Haiti, first in 1980, and multiple times since then. Over the years, the Seabecks have also shipped more than a million pounds of goods to this devastatingly poor nation.

The couple's ministry is not limited to Haiti though. With their own money and donations from others, they've built churches in Honduras and Sudan, and helped furnish over 20 chapels for Mother Teresa's nuns throughout the Caribbean.

But it's their hands-on time with the poor that means the most. "With what we do," says Ray, "we see a difference in people's lives."

A loving heart in action makes all the difference in the world.

Has not God chosen the poor in the world to be rich in faith and to be heirs of the kingdom that He has promised to those who love Him? (James 2:5)

In the eyes of the poor, I see Your face, calling me to love in Your name, Lord.

Signs of the Times

Rev. Duane Pribula of the Crookston, Minnesota, Catholic diocese admits that he's not an economist. Still, after observing the signs of the times, he offers some worthwhile advice:

- Talk with your teens and younger children about the financial pressures on your family, neighbors, the nation, the world.
- Don't live simply so your children can live lavishly; as a family survey your financial situation and establish real limits.
- Insist that each family member becomes economical, even frugal in lifestyle.
- Consolidate and eliminate debts as quickly as possible.
- Cut all unnecessary expenses.
- Decrease usage of energy and processed foods.
- Discuss practical birthday and Christmas gifts.
- Be as generous with food pantries, soup kitchens, used clothing drives as possible.

You know how to interpret the appearance of the sky, but you cannot interpret the signs of the times....No sign will be given...except the sign of Jonah. (Matthew 16:3,4)

God, help us interpret the signs of the times wisely and courageously, with self reliance.

A Woman and an Architect

Louise Blanchard Bethune began as a draftsman for Waite and Caulkins, a Buffalo, New York, architectural firm in 1876. She opened her own architectural practice in 1881 and designed industrial, commercial and educational buildings in Buffalo until 1912.

Bethune was elected to membership in the American Institute of Architects in 1888; and became its first woman Fellow the next year.

Bethune said that women "should be judged on" their "capabilities not gender." She also said that women "pioneers in any profession should be proficient in every department. Women architects must be practical superintendents, designers and scientific constructors." She also advocated "equal remuneration for equal service."

When education or employment is restricted because of gender, age or race the world is impoverished.

I commend to you...Phoebe, a deacon of the church at Cenchreae...Mary, who has worked very hard among you...and Junia...prominent among the apostles. (Romans 16:1,6,7)

Holy Wisdom, remind us that discrimination offends You, the Creator of every human being.

The Silver Lining in Failure

Writer Valerie Schultz saw herself as a reasonably successful person with a thriving, long-term marriage, four healthy daughters and a steady flow of projects for her freelance business.

Then she decided to play it safe and take a teaching job for more secure income. Soon she realized she was doing it for the wrong reasons. Her work and her students began to suffer.

A fellow teacher said that "No one goes into teaching for the money. If that's why you're here, you should not be a teacher." Schultz knew her colleague was right. Then she failed two courses she was taking to earn her credentials and found herself unequipped to deal with failure.

But her "initial horror gave way to a creeping sense of peace," she says. She found the experience strengthened her, filling her with humility and a renewed devotion to prayer and reliance on God.

With God's grace, find the positive in difficult situations!

Take My yoke upon you, and learn from me; for I am gentle and humble in heart, and you will find rest for your souls. (Matthew 11:29)

Strengthen me, Abba.

Waiting on the Sun

Once a year, the residents of Longyearbyen, Norway, get ready for the return of their friend—the sun! You see, total darkness blankets the area from mid-November through January! In February, the sun is well below the horizon; daytime has only indirect light. But then the sun climbs closer to the horizon until one day in early March it rises for the first time since October.

Schoolchildren prepare artwork and songs in praise of the sun's return. The day is a public holiday. Residents of this remote Arctic settlement observe that with the sun's return, energy levels and their spirits, in general rise. But others feel a twinge of regret, finding the darkness a time for contemplation and for slowing down life's hectic pace.

As the sun has its alternating cycles, so our lives should have a healthful alternation of reflection and of action.

By the tender mercy of our God, the dawn from on high will break upon us, to give light to those who sit in darkness and in the shadow of death. (Luke 1:78-79)

Light of the world, may we reflect Your light to others.

A Multidimensional Man

Most know Herbie Hancock as the Grammy-winning musician whose mentor was jazz great Miles Davis. But there's much more to him.

In an interview, Hancock said that after years of studying the piano, he wasn't open "to jazz until high school, but when I was, it just overtook me."

He also discussed his reaction to the loss of his sister, who was killed in a plane crash. "I didn't cry for six months, but when we threw her ashes to sea, the tears came, finally," he admits.

Ultimately, Hancock emphasized his belief that human beings are not just one-dimensional. "I'm a musician, a father, a husband, a son, a citizen, a friend, an American, an African American and at the root, a human being," he said.

How glorious and beautiful must our Creator be, if we and the rest of creation are so complex and wonderful!

For from the greatness and beauty of created things comes a corresponding perception of their Creator. (Wisdom of Solomon 13:5)

I celebrate my beautiful humanity, a gift from You, Beauty ever ancient, ever new.

A Basis for Life

Having turned 50, author Amy Bloom was asked by *AARP* Magazine to reflect on what the years had taught her. She offered these thoughts:

Forgive. "Since disappointments and misunderstandings are inevitable," Bloom says, "I've become a huge fan of forgiving people who act badly." She also favors apologizing for wrongs done.

Face reality. "I don't want to pretend that bad things are not happening when they are," she explains. Dealing with tough problems and bad times is part of life, Bloom observes.

Value time. "People who say time is money are wrong," she says. "Time is better than money, and I want as much as I possibly can have." She stresses especially paying attention to those around you, and spending time with those you love.

Life is a gift; treasure the lessons life teaches us.

Trust in the Lord with all your heart. ...In all your ways acknowledge Him. ...Do not be wise in your own eyes...and turn away from evil. (Proverbs 3:5,6,7)

Help me to see, Lord, the goodness around me and the good You want me to do.

Love Cures All

As Ann awoke from surgery, her mind still clouded from anesthesia and pain, she found herself focusing on the activity in her hospital room.

The young woman who was her roommate was severely disabled and in need of constant care. Ann watched as her mother assisted her. She also witnessed the staff's seemingly endless patience and boundless compassion.

Noticing that Ann was awake, the mother came to her bedside, asking if she needed anything. Ann was touched, and thanked her for the concern.

In that moment, a feeling of hope washed over Ann, the hope that comes from remembering that love, God's love most of all, is always around us. We just need to open our eyes and our hearts to let it in to heal us.

> **Jesus said, "Someone touched Me; for I noticed that power had gone out from Me."...she declared...why she had touched Him..."Daughter, your faith has made you well; go in peace." (Luke 8:46,47,48)**

Send me Your healing love, Divine Master.

Mission — Connection

Bishop Dunne Catholic High School in Dallas, Texas, is one of four in that city where young people can participate in a summer mission trip to Honduras. Combining service and education, students are involved with specific projects and also explore Honduras and its culture.

"We are building solidarity with our Honduran brothers and sisters," says Lydia Torrez, trip coordinator and director of development at Bishop Dunne H.S.

"I saw the faith of the Honduran people and I was inspired," says senior Riley Emmons.

"We worked together, but even more importantly we formed relationships," offers student Christina Gleason.

Connecting, across miles or just with a neighbor at work or at home enriches lives in both directions.

(Jesus) made His home in Capernaum...so that what had been spoken through the prophet Isaiah might be fulfilled: "...the people who sat in darkness have seen a great light." (Matthew 4:13,14,16)

Help me build bridges of understanding and sow seeds of love and kindness, Jesus.

The Forest and the Trees

You know the expression, "You can't see the forest for the trees." Well, do you ever feel that you cannot see your whole life for all your days?

We get so caught up in "the daily grind" that we lose sight of what's important. And what's important isn't only big moments, like weddings, births and other life-altering changes. What's important is little moments that we can't see because we're blinded by negative attitudes and pressures we put on ourselves.

Robert Louis Stevenson had some good advice: "The day dawns and brings us another petty round of irritating concerns and duties. Help us to perform them with laughter and kind faces. Let cheerfulness abound with industry. Let us go blithely about our business all this day, bring us to our resting beds weary, content, not dishonored, and grant us in the end the gift of sleep."

Find simple joys for yourself and to share with others.

The precepts of the Lord are right, rejoicing the heart. (Psalm 19:8)

Generous God, thank You for my life. Show me how to live it well to glorify You and for my own sake and the sake of those around me.

More than a Souper Bowl

Each year football fans watch the top two NFL teams compete in the Super Bowl. Family and friends gather to have fun over abundant cold cuts, cheese, ribs, chili, potato chips, dips, salsas, beer and soda and more!

It's also a good day to think of others: 35 million Americans are food insecure and 45 per cent of U.S. cities can not meet citizens' basic food needs.

Back in 1990, youth groups at 22 churches in Columbia, South Carolina, raised $5,700 in the Souper Bowl of Caring. Since then, $50 million has been donated to soup kitchens and food banks across the country through this expanding project.

Encourage your church youth group to celebrate Super Bowl Sunday by remembering the hungry; and to select a local group working with needy people as the recipient of your sharing and caring. Enhance your joyful celebration. Remember those without even a bowl of soup to eat.

When you give a banquet, invite the poor, the crippled, the lame, and the blind. And...you will be repaid at the resurrection of the righteous. (Luke 14:13-14)

Help us express our gratitude by our generosity, God.

Rock and Roll Really Is Here to Stay

The 1960s in America were known for a lot of things, but perhaps most prominently its music. Many baby boomers who came of age then still yearn to connect with their music.

Las Vegas' Rock and Roll Fantasy Camp seeks to make some fans' dream a reality. They can spend up to five days practicing in bona fide rehearsal studios with once celebrated or still-famous rock musicians preparing for a mock-rock concert.

But clients spend more than time to hang out with their rock and roll idols. The thrill of performing with the band of their dreams costs aficionados as much as $10,000! Those who can afford the indulgence say it's worth it: one devotee remarked after the experience, "I couldn't get to sleep until 3:00 am."

Living out a fantasy is one way to connect with a long-lost passion. Volunteering is another. Explore volunteer opportunities in your area. They may offer a path to true fulfillment and joy.

Everyone then who hears these words of Mine and acts on them will be like a wise man who built his house on rock. (Matthew 7:24)

Remind me how truly simple it is to help make the world a better place, Merciful Savior.

Conservation Suggestions

The Quintanas and Max, their Labrador, from Tucson, Arizona, and the Flood family from Cedarburg, Wisconsin, offered these conservation suggestions in *Family Circle* magazine:

1. Conserve water when brushing your teeth, showering, shaving; using the clothes washer.
2. Use water-conserving native plants in your yard.
3. Compost kitchen scraps for use in your garden.
4. Buy secondhand clothes for daily use.
5. Use the moisture-sensor on the clothes dryer.
6. Write supporting fuel standards and clean air and water regulations.
7. Use reusable nylon or canvas shopping bags.
8. Write the Direct Marketing Association or go to catalogchoice.org to be removed from mass market lists.
9. Turn off the lights when leaving a room.
10. Walk. Bike. Carpool. Use public transit.

God made us stewards of His Earth. Be a good one.

It is required of stewards that they be found trustworthy. (1 Corinthians 4:2)

Inspire our stewardship of Your Earth which You have given us as our home, Creator.

Sweet Dreams

Keeping a bouquet of sweet-smelling flowers near your bed just might help you have pleasant dreams.

Researchers in Germany tested volunteers while they slept, giving some the scent of roses and others, a whiff of rotten eggs. Then they woke them up and those who had smelled flowers had experienced enjoyable dreams. Those who smelled the rotten eggs didn't have nightmares about smells or tastes, but their dreams were generally negative and disturbing.

Tim Jacob, an expert in smell and taste at Cardiff University says, "Smell is the only sense that doesn't 'sleep'. Information continues to reach the limbic system of the brain that is involved with emotional response."

The human body is amazingly complex. Let's enjoy and celebrate God's gift to us and use it well.

Better off poor, healthy, and fit than rich and afflicted in body. (Sirach 30:14)

Help us to appreciate this wonderful body You've bestowed on us and the mind You've also given us, Generous Father.

Finding Alone Time

When was the last time you had two full hours of uninterrupted time, all to yourself? If you're like most people, your day may be so busy that you might not have time to ponder such a question.

Writer Kyle T. Kramer remembers how his days were once so busy that he barely had time to pray. He struggled constantly to nurture his relationship with God, while juggling his responsibilities. How many of us can truly relate to that statement!

Kramer grew fruits and vegetables for market on his 27-acre farm, while raising three children. His day began at 5 a.m. Kramer viewed the first two hours as "alone time," often spent praying, thinking or planning for his and his family's future. In fact, those two hours soon became an integral part of his day.

Even five minutes of solitude can help refresh a tired soul. Serenity can be found in the most unlikely of places, too.

Come away to a deserted place all by yourselves and rest a while. (Mark 6:31)

Soothe my weary spirit, Counselor. Teach me how to enter into silence and solitude anywhere, anytime.

Like a Box of Chocolates

Because she thinks that we can find life's lessons in candy, Sister Judy Gomila sends friends and family sweet treats, with a note about how each speaks to everyday reality. Here are some of this New Orleans native's insights:

Nestlé Crunch® — Life is good, even if it isn't always smooth.

Peppermint Patty® — Remember to stay cool in stressful times.

Tootsie® Roll — Take it one day at a time; roll with the punches.

Milky Way® — Aim high and reach for the stars, day after day.

Snickers® — Take life seriously, but wear it lightly, smile!

Life is always filled with sweet moments to treasure.

(Ravens) neither sow nor reap, they have neither storehouse nor barn, and yet God feeds them...Lilies...neither toil nor spin; yet...even Solomon...was not clothed like (them). (Luke 12:24,27)

You offer us all good things, Lord. May our actions always offer You praise.

Having a Heart for Others

Jane Moore was having a hard time dealing with the death of her husband of 35 years. Then, one day in February, she got an invitation for a Sweetheart Banquet to be held at the local Baptist church.

The men of the church had decided to have a special dinner for the widows in their Coalfield, Tennessee, community. Moore and the other guests were given corsages and enjoyed a lovely dinner. They even received Valentine Day cards prepared by schoolchildren. The evening has become a tradition.

"It's a blessing to live in a community where people truly care," says Moore in *Guideposts* magazine.

Encourage your neighbors to find ways to aid and comfort those in your community who are lonely or in need. It could make a great difference to someone else and to you.

Encourage one another. (1 Thessalonians 4:18)

Holy Trinity, open my eyes and my heart to those around me and help me to show them Your love.

What Love Is—and Isn't

Every single human being has been given the ability to love by God Himself. Whether or not we use this gift is up to us, but here are some considerations worth pondering:

- Love delights in giving attention rather than in attracting it.
- Love finds the element of good in others and builds on it. It does not magnify defects.
- Love lets you see the other person's point of view even when you cannot embrace it.
- Love can disagree without being disagreeable.
- Love strives to make a bad situation better instead of merely griping about it.
- Love avoids causing unnecessary pain. It does not scorn, ridicule or belittle. It tactfully inspires faith, hope and charity.

Fill your life with acts of love for God, your self and God's children. Remember that life is a journey into the arms of our loving God.

"You shall not commit adultery; You shall not murder; You shall not steal; You shall not covet"; and any other commandment are summed up in..."Love your neighbor as yourself." (Romans 13:9)

Never let me grow weary of serving You, Loving God, by loving others as I love my self.

In a Word, a Nation Preserved

Some historians believe that in order to really *know* Abraham Lincoln, we must look past the ways in which we remember him.

We remember Lincoln as the president who ended slavery. Yet, there's so much more to him than that. Complex, contradictory, often depressed and fiercely committed to a unified United States, Lincoln was born and raised on the harsh frontier. Torn between two incompatible social systems, he once defended slavery, then initiated its demise. He had a hearty sense of humor, but was mirthless about the attempt to divide this country.

Perhaps the real Lincoln is symbolized by a telling but obscure fact: by the time of Lincoln's assassination people no longer said "the United States *are*," but rather, "the United States *is*."

Imitate Lincoln by seeking, as he said, "malice toward none; charity for all."

For freedom Christ has set us free...Do not submit again to a yoke of slavery. (Galatians 5:1)

Remind us, Great Healer, that if even one person is enslaved then all are enslaved. May we work for freedom and equality under the law for all.

"Dog Man" — A Tale of Enduring Values

Usually people train dogs. But Morie Sawataishi has been taught by his Akitas. One especially, named Samurai Tiger, "was natural, raw and unspoiled," notes Sawataishi. "For me, he was everything I could ask for in a dog. He had all the traits I hoped to someday see in myself."

An ancient Japanese breed, the Akita had by 1944 nearly been killed off. Then Sawataishi brought them back. An engineer for Mitsubishi, he and his wife left cosmopolitan Tokyo for the mountains of Japan's snow country to breed and show these prized and loyal animals.

A *Newsweek* magazine review of his biography, *Dog Man* by Martha Sherrill, says the story about Sawataishi "and his magnificent dogs—with their superior intelligence, stamina, fearlessness and almost spiritual calm—is really about the search for enduring values."

For those who are open to the experience life's lessons can come from unexpected sources.

Every wild animal...and all domestic animals... and every creeping thing...and every bird...went into the ark with Noah, two and two of all flesh in which there was the breath of life. (Genesis 7:14,15)

Thank You, Creator, for the gift of companion animals.

It's Time to Lent

Do you Lent?

Dolores Curran, who writes on family and spiritual issues, told a story in her book, *Family Prayer* about a young boy who taught her something about Lent. When Curran visited friends, little Tony showed her a Lenten calendar, which was similar to an Advent calendar. "Every night we get to open a door," he said.

"And what do you do then?" Curran asked.

"Oh, we Lent!" he answered.

"I've never heard Lent used as a verb, but it's a perfect use for it because it is an action word," writes Curran. She goes on to say that Lent is "a time for spiritual renewal of self, family and parish." It's an opportunity for families and the larger community to pray and observe rituals that can help us grow in spirit.

This year, consider ways that you and your family and even your church can do more to use Lent to nurture your souls.

Rend your hearts and not your clothing. Return to...your God, for He is gracious and merciful, slow to anger, and abounding in steadfast love. (Joel 2:13)

Spirit of Grace, help us to grow, to thrive, to flourish in Your Presence.

The Unscheduled Life

According to experts there's such a thing as too planned. Even if planning saves one's sanity while getting things accomplished, you can overdo it. In fact, your health and happiness could be in jeopardy, your life more stressful and less spontaneous if every minute is scheduled. According to *Body + Soul Magazine* there are remedies:

- Consider your schedule as a sketch which allows you to go with the flow when you want to.

- Vary such routines as your route to work; where you walk or jog; or where you buy your morning coffee or newspaper.

- Remember that you have an obligation to yourself. Scheduled chores will wait if there's something you'd really rather do.

- Say "yes" to spur-of-the minute invitations. Meet new people, enjoy new experiences.

- Do what's adventurous, challenging and pleasing every once in a while.

You have one God-given life. Live!

There is nothing better for (workers) than to be happy and enjoy themselves as long as they live. (Ecclesiastes 3:12)

Blessed Trinity, teach us spontaneity, relaxation, and adventurousness.

Plastic and the Environment

We've read that plastic does not decompose for at least years, even centuries, harming our environment. Tons of garbage and toxic, long-lasting wastes are the result.

Recycline, a New York City based company, is trying to combat plastics' deleterious effects on our world and our health by recycling plastics into toothbrushes, razors, colanders, cutting boards and other personal-care and household items. This helps cut costs for consumers while bringing a much-needed respite to our trash-burdened environment.

Says Eric Hudson, Recycline's founder and a devoted environmentalist, "customers are part of our supply chain. People recycle yogurt cups, and they help make kitchen items."

Recycling is more than trendy, it is essential in restoring our own health and the health of our environment. What can you do to restore our Earth to vigorous health?

May the Lord rejoice in His works — who looks on the earth and it trembles, who touches the mountains and they smoke. (Psalm 104:31-32)

Bless our efforts at the restoration and conservation of the Earth, Creator of all.

What Became of Paper and Ink?

For some of us growing up in the 20th century, an ordinary, hardcover dictionary was an important shaper of our general education as well as our specific use of language.

One of the best known, then and now, is the Oxford English Dictionary, or O.E.D. Replete with onion-skin pages and semi-circle indents for each letter of the alphabet, each edition included a supplemental update, a practice that Oxford began in 1933.

Today, most of what is contained in a print version of the O.E.D. can be found in cyberspace. Lexicographers upload their revisions to each edition of the dictionary online. Efficient? Of course. But for some of us, nothing will ever replace the magnificent, bulky and intricate paper version of an English-speaker's treasure.

Continue to learn, using whatever tools are at your disposal.

The memory of the righteous is a blessing. (Proverbs 10:7)

Enable me to hold onto those worthwhile traditions and wholesome memories that I hold dear, Jesus.

A Bill and a Prayer

Jan Weeks dreaded her bills. Her teacher's salary barely covered them and worrying about them seemed less daunting than actually paying them.

Then her sister sent her inspirational tapes that spoke about appreciating life and its blessings.

So Weeks tried a different approach. Instead of dreading her bills, she began to bless them. As she wrote the check for the utility bill, she prayed for all who kept her warm. As she sent a payment to the telephone company, she gave thanks because she was able to stay in touch with people she loved. Within a few weeks, her debts, although the same, now seemed more manageable.

It's always best to put things in perspective and to remember that life is God's great gift to each one of us.

With gratitude in your hearts sing...to God...in the name of the Lord Jesus, giving thanks to God the Father through Him.
(Colossians 3:16,17)

For all who labor for others' good, Lord, we offer a prayer of gratitude.

Inspired Decisions

In the book of Proverbs (16:10) inspired decisions are said to be "on the lips of a king." And while you're not a king or queen, you can still make inspired decisions. Some suggestions:

- Pray. Ask to see the truth of your motives. Ask to be led in the right way for yourself and your loved ones.

- If you are tired or under pressure, do not make significant decisions, emergencies excepted. Catch your breath, review the facts and only then decide.

- Prioritize your decisions. Some are more urgent.

- When making business decisions talk to business people and colleagues. Talk to your spouse, too.

- Consult with your spouse and your children when making family decisions.

Whether they are major or minor, strive to make the best choices you can.

Search me, O God, and know my heart; test me and know my thoughts...and lead me in the way everlasting. (Psalm 139:23,24)

Inspire my smallest decisions, Holy Wisdom.

Mother to Hundreds

Growing up, Anurak Chiayaphuek recalls her feelings as her friends married and started families. "My heart wanted more," she says. "I became a Religious Sister to give God's love to everyone."

Since 1996, she and other Good Shepherd Sisters in her native Thailand have operated homes for girls in need. "We take in every girl who comes to us," Sister Anurak explains. "God loves all and we should as well."

Some of the girls have lost parents through illness or violence, while others have been rescued from human trafficking and slavery. The Sisters also go into the villages, running HIV/AIDS and trafficking awareness programs.

"My family numbers in the hundreds now," Sister Anurak says. "My heart now overflows with gratitude."

Married, unmarried, widowed, vowed sister or brother, ordained deacon, minister or priest, led by love of God and neighbor, we can work miracles for those around us.

Serve one another with whatever gift each of you has received. (1 Peter 4:10)

With great joy, I share Your love with others, Father, knowing that You share Your love with me.

Having a Positive Attitude

Isaac Bashevis Singer wrote, "If you keep on saying things are going to be bad, you have a good chance of becoming a prophet." So how can you choose not to become a prophet of doom?

Communicate your genuine feelings rather than feel frustration, hurt, anger or anxiety. Limit your exposure to negative news and find more positive things to do with your precious time.

Allow yourself to be loved and to love. Find humor in the simplest of things. Read some jokes. Watch a funny movie. Act "silly."

Listen to your internal dialogue and rewrite negative thoughts positively. Get back to basics because the simplest things in life give us the most pleasure. Develop your spirituality in worship with others and alone.

Singer himself would never say that it's easy to be always positive. But you and your life are worth the effort.

In the case of an athlete, no one is crowned without competing according to the rules. (2 Timothy 2:5)

Gracious God, help me approach each moment of each hour of each day filled with hopefulness.

A Wealth of Weather History

People have climbed to the National Weather Service's station near the upstate New York Mohonk Mountain House resort for 112 years. Since the hotel opened, weather observers have recorded local temperatures and weather conditions, and recurring natural events, such as bird migrations and foliage trends.

The recorders also recorded a wealth of local history, as well as insight into larger trends and shifts in weather patterns. Their data offers today's scientists intriguing indicators on overall climate change and its effects. Some of the data may, for example, be useful in gauging and forecasting global warming trends. Yet, those who recorded the information likely had no idea their notations would assist researchers decades later.

Every act you undertake to help others makes a difference. No effort to assist others is ever wasted.

Do not grieve the hungry, or anger one in need. Do not add to the troubles of the desperate, or delay giving to the needy. ...Their Creator will hear their prayer. (Sirach 4:2-3,6)

Jesus of Nazareth, help us be frugal so that there will be more for our needy sisters and brothers.

Help Me!

Does your family feel that you can do it all, or that you don't want their assistance? Well, there are ways to get help.

- No nagging. Communicate about what you need in an honest, non-blaming way.
- Call a meeting. Gather family members to discuss the big picture and find a solution together.
- Spell it out. Make your requests for assistance specific.
- Be needy. Help others understand that they are important, not only in accomplishing tasks, but also in caring for your well-being.
- Be quiet. Once you've followed these steps, stand back and let others do what you've asked. Don't criticize or hover or you may not get such help again.

Above all, always be grateful. Acknowledge the gift of time and talent offered to you, out of love, with a return of loving thanks.

Be thankful. (Colossians 3:15)

Grateful praise is Yours, Master, for always providing what I need.

Cartoons and Potato Chips

For nearly a month, there didn't seem to be a second of rest for Maggie. Long work days ran into evenings of things to do at home for her husband and family.

Then on the one night she planned to just relax, an emergency with her pregnant daughter-in-law added another "to-do" to her already over-flowing list. She had to baby-sit her three-year-old grandson, Jake.

Resigned to an evening of running around, she soon found out that Jake only wanted to sit on the couch, watch cartoons and snack on Maggie's favorite treat sour cream and onion potato chips. Soon, Maggie had an unusual feeling come over her—peace and quiet, interrupted occasionally by grandma and grandson crunching chips.

Relief from our trials and worries can sometimes mean opening our hearts to another's good idea.

You are the God in whom I take refuge; why have you cast me off? Why must I walk about mournfully? (Psalm 43:2)

Clothe me, Eternal One, with Your love and peace.

Give — No Matter What

No doubt you have heard of Anne Frank and the diary she kept while she and her family hid from the Nazis for two years. And you probably know that after they were captured, Anne and most of the others died in concentration camps.

In addition to the diary, she wrote a number of other things including an essay called "Give." Here's an excerpt:

"How wonderful it is that no one has to wait, but can start right now to gradually change the world! How wonderful it is that everyone, great and small, can immediately help bring about justice by giving of themselves! Give whatever there is to give! You can always give something, even if it's a simple act of kindness!"

While her faith and hope could not save her life, they gave her a legacy beyond her imaginings. She kept giving through her words. How will you give today?

Be...generous. (1 Timothy 6:18)

Remind me to give love and justice and mercy each hour of life You give me, gracious Lord.

Against All Odds

In Tallassee, Alabama, during the 1930s "it seemed like the textile mills in town were laying off workers every day," Georgia Moon writes. Just before her senior year of high school, her own father lost his job. So she went to work to ensure that she would be able to attend her class's senior trip to the famed Tuskegee Institute.

She was fascinated with the life story of the university's celebrated plant scientist Dr. George Washington Carver and wanted to meet him.

Born a slave in Missouri, Dr. Carver became one of the few American members of England's Royal Society for the Encouragement of the Arts. Asked by a student where he found his many ideas for improving agriculture, he remarked, "God gave the ideas to me."

After meeting Dr. Carver, Moon knew she had met "a truly great man."

Human beings are still enslaved. Work for human rights.

God created humankind in His image...male and female He created them. (Genesis 1:27)

Open the eyes of those who do not see that they share a common humanity with those whom they oppress, Just Judge.

Get Out and Bike!

It's no secret that childhood obesity is a worsening national problem. According to the Washington Post, 15 per cent of six- to 15-year olds are now considered overweight or obese, twice the number two decades ago.

But the problem doesn't end with childhood. Overweight children are more likely than their slimmer peers to be overweight or even obese adults. One of the reasons for rising child obesity is families' increasingly sedentary lives. Passive activities, such as video games and television viewing, are particular culprits.

A non-profit group, Trips for Kids, works nationwide to encourage biking among children, hoping to foster healthy exercise routines and promote healthy weight loss.

Children deserve a healthy start in life. Set a healthful standard for your children. Participate in regular, moderate physical activity with your family.

Every year His parents went to Jerusalem for the festival of the Passover. (Luke 2:41)

Jesus, whose family annually walked more than 90 miles from Nazareth to Jerusalem and back, help parents respect and strengthen their bodies and teach their children to do the same.

Only God Could Have Made a Tree!

Diana Beresford-Kroeger believes trees can save humankind. Beresford-Kroeger, who holds degrees in medical biochemistry and botany, and has worked as a researcher at the University of Ottawa's School of Medicine, sees trees as complex, unique and potentially healing.

Take the towering wafer ash tree which is a virtual chemical factory. Its flowers contain terpene oils, which repel flower-eating mammals. But to attract pollinators for its flowers, the wafer ash's flowers have a powerful fragrance that appeals to butterflies and honeybees. These chemicals, in turn, protect the butterflies from birds by making the butterflies taste bitter.

This tree's unique and powerful chemical properties could be applied to organic farming, bio-planning and natural medicines.

All of this potential, from just one tree!

No wonder that God's power and scope in Creation is hard for us to comprehend. Nevertheless, try to grow in appreciation.

God said, "Let the earth put forth...fruit trees of every kind...that bear fruit with the seed in it." And it was so. ...And God saw that it was good. (Genesis 1:11,12)

How great and powerful is our God! How wonderful are the works of God's hands!

Better to Light One Candle

The Christopher motto that "It's better to light one candle than to curse the darkness" means many things to many people. To business owners and managers it can be a reminder that they and their corporations can make a positive difference. Here are some ideas from The Woodstock Theological Center:

- Have a purpose and goals that serve the larger community.
- Be concerned about the impact of actions.
- Avoid deception and misrepresentation of facts.
- Keep commitments with competence and quality.
- Distribute burdens and benefits equally.
- Avoid improper influences or conflicts of interest and be loyal in executing managerial duties.
- Be fair, honest and reliable with individuals. Respect individual autonomy and privacy.
- Exercise care with tangible property, patents, confidential information and real estate.

Ethical companies are a necessary pillar of society.

Set an example. (Judith 8:24)

Encourage owners, managers and employees of corporations to set an example of principled behavior, Wisdom.

A New Vision

James Holman's dream to see the world was shattered when he lost his vision in his mid-twenties. But the young British Royal Navy officer's passion for travel remained intact. In fact, he was destined to become known as "The Blind Explorer."

Defying expectations, Holman, who was born in 1786, set off on a series of adventures that ultimately took him from England to Siberia, Africa, South America, Australia, India, Turkey and the Middle East.

Holman blazed new trails and was an inspiration to others. He also proved, contrary to then popular belief, that being blind did not mean being helpless or mentally impaired.

Most of us can see, even if eyeglasses are necessary. But discrimination and prejudice against those with limited or no vision remains. What can you do to make life more respect-filled for blind people and those with impaired sight?

You shall not revile the deaf or put a stumbling block before the blind; you shall fear your God: I am the Lord. (Leviticus 19:14)

Help us to respect the human dignity of people with disabilities, Holy Spirit.

What You Hear and What You Eat

Is your love of music interfering with your diet? "Adults eat and drink more when there's background noise," according to Nanette Stroebele of the University of Colorado's Center for Human Nutrition writing in *AARP* magazine.

Some studies even conclude that the louder and faster the music, the more people eat. While softer music slows down your rate of chewing and aids digestion, it also encourages diners to linger. That leads to overeating. Eating while watching TV is also a problem because it tends to delay the signal between the stomach and the brain that let's people know they're full.

Instead, engage in quiet conversation, use soft lighting and breathe between bites to slow down eating. And be sure to chew food well to release an enzyme that encourages carbohydrates to be used as fuel rather than stored.

Taking good care of your health is vital to your overall well-being. Make the effort today.

Health and fitness are better than any gold, and a robust body than countless riches. (Sirach 30:15)

Holy Creator, remind me to look after myself and my loved ones physically, mentally and spiritually.

Simply Powerful

On one particular Sunday, Pauline seemed to feel more deeply the devastating loss of her husband who had died only months earlier.

After Sunday services, she decided to head straight home, instead of joining her friends at their usual early dinner.

As she stepped into her apartment, Pauline was overcome by sadness. She started to cry, her sobbing interrupted by a knock at the door. It was her friend Jane. She had followed Pauline home, deciding to skip dinner with the group as well.

"Let's just sit for a while," Jane told Pauline, "and I'll hold your hand." And the two did just that.

A simple gesture, a loving touch, a listening ear, a reassuring smile—can make a powerful difference for someone in need.

Moved with compassion, Jesus touched their eyes. Immediately they regained their sight and followed Him. (Matthew 20:34)

Jesus, show me where You need me to bring Your loving touch today.

The Habit of Virtue

Virtue, which is basically the habit of performing actions for good, is not a term we hear much about these days. Yet that does not mean we cannot develop virtues.

The Markkula Center for Applied Ethics at California's Santa Clara University says that virtue ethics provides for "the full development of our humanity. These virtues are dispositions and habits that enable us to act according to the highest potential of our character and on behalf of values like…honesty, courage, compassion, generosity, tolerance, love, fidelity, integrity, self-control, and prudence.

"Virtue ethics asks of any action, 'What kind of person will I become if I do this?' or 'Is this action consistent with my acting my best?'"

People cannot grow in virtue without applying themselves in small daily matters as well as major decisions. One day at a time, just do your best, and pray for the rest.

Choose this day whom you will serve. (Joshua 24:15)

Let me rely on You, Gracious God, to put Your grace to good work within me.

Communing with Nature

Ever wonder if today's youngsters take enough time flipping over rocks looking for salamanders? OK, you probably haven't. But Patricia Riexinger, Director of New York State's Division of Fish, Wildlife and Marine Resources, a wildlife biologist and a Girl Scout leader, does.

She says that "people losing contact with the natural world" is one of the greatest threats to conservation. So Riexinger wants the public to spend time outdoors experiencing the sense of wonder awaiting them.

"Most kids, when they think of outdoor recreation, think of playing soccer on a mowed field, or maybe of a basketball court in an asphalt world," Riexinger told the *New York Times*. "We're poorer as a people, emotionally and ethically if we don't have some connection to and respect for the natural world."

Introduce yourself, a loved one, children, to the natural world's fierce wild loveliness, wisdom and seasonality.

Praise Him, sun and moon...shining stars ...deeps, fire and hail, snow and frost, stormy wind...mountains...hills, fruit trees...cedars! Wild animals...cattle, creeping things and flying birds! (Psalm 148:3,7-8,9-10)

Thank You for Your world, Creator of all.

Needs that Hurt

If someone is described as self-destructive, you might envision a person with serious alcohol or drug problems. But people can also hurt themselves by their own unhealthy needs:

- The need to be always right.
- The need to be first in everything.
- The need to be constantly in control.
- The need to be perfect.
- The need to be loved by everyone.
- The need to possess.
- The need to be free of conflict and frustration.
- The need to change others.
- The need to manipulate.

It's not easy to change our habits or way of thinking, but by being more gentle and loving with ourselves and others, we can lead happier, more positive lives.

Jesus answered, "...love the Lord your God with all your heart...soul...mind, and...strength...love your neighbor as yourself. There is no other commandment greater than these." (Mark 12:29,30,31)

Merciful Savior, help me to see myself and my neighbors with Your loving eyes.

A Circle of Giving

A few dollars, a few friends and a little commitment can make a big difference. Ericka Carter and some friends were troubled by the world's problems and, wanting to make a change, began the San Fernando Valley Giving Circle. They meet every other month and contribute $10.00 each.

That may not sound like much. But Carter says that when she "delivered food coupons to a struggling young mother," she was told "please ask other people to do this too, because we usually get help only at Christmas."

Across America, giving circles have become very popular—12,000 people have joined these groups and raised nearly $100 million. A circle in Reston, Virginia, helps low-income neighbors, the homeless and the elderly. A large one in Seattle, Washington, has awarded millions to social-service organizations.

By joining with others you can make a great difference for others today.

Be rich in good works. (1 Timothy 6:18)

Inspire many to pool their resources for the common good, Holy Redeemer.

Parents and their Children

Most parents work hard to raise their children with love and respect for them as individuals. Sadly there are exceptions.

Lisa shoved her newborn away screaming, "I wanted a boy!" Now she tells the 8-year-old that raising her costs too much.

When Joe, Jr. says he wants to be a commercial artist, his dentist dad says he needs to grow up and be a man.

Laurie insists that her toddler, Phil, be slim. She withholds food and punishes him for wailing with hunger.

Bill is still angry that his adult son, Tom, refused to be the priest Bill wanted him to be before he married.

Sue regularly reminds her teenaged daughter that she must be the high school principal Sue never became.

How can you help immature parents accept and nurture the children—made in God's image and likeness—that they have?

If there anyone among you who, if your child asks for a fish, will give a snake instead? ...Or...for an egg, will give a scorpion? (Luke 11:11,12)

Jesus, protect children from psychological, spiritual or physical abuse.

Hero Dogs

While serving in Vietnam, U.S. Marine Ron Aiello's life was saved by his partner Stormy, a German Shepherd. Stormy stopped and heeled, alerting Aiello that something wasn't right. Moments later, a sniper opened fire, just missing him.

In the time they were together, Aiello adds, Stormy saved his life a few times. Aiello, now president of the non-profit United States War Dogs Association, estimates that military dogs saved about 10,000 lives in Vietnam, and have saved thousands in Iraq and Afghanistan as well. Dogs on duty detect land mines and explosives, conduct search and rescue operations, and serve as guard dogs.

It's often those beside us, loyal, loving friends and family, and, yes, companion animals, who make all the difference in our life's everyday struggles.

Whoever walks with the wise becomes wise, but the companion of fools suffers harm. (Proverbs 13:20)

I search for You in the darkness, Father. Reveal Your light to me.

If...

The late humorist and author Erma Bombeck penned these thoughts when she learned she'd survived breast cancer only to face polycystic kidney disease and a kidney transplant:

"I would have talked less and listened more; especially when Grandfather rambled about his youth.

"I would have invited friends over to dinner even if the carpet was stained, or the sofa faded.

"I would have cried and laughed less while watching television and more while watching life.

"I would never have bought anything just because it was practical, wouldn't show soil, or ...(would) last a lifetime.

"I would have shared more of the responsibility carried by my husband.

"I would seize every minute...look at it and really see it...live it and never give it back."

Life is God's gift. Show your gratitude by living your unique life to its moment-by-moment fullest.

Remember your Creator in the days of your youth, before the days...when you will say, "I have no pleasure in them." (Ecclesiastes 12:1)

God, enable me to plunge into life unreservedly.

Do What You Love — Success Will Follow

There are people who work to live, and others who live to work. Science-fiction novelist Ray Bradbury serves as an example of the latter.

As an octogenarian Bradbury admits that love is what compels and fuels his drive to write. He loves so passionately, that even after a stroke paralyzed part of his right side, he didn't stop writing. His thirtieth book was released recently, followed soon after by his fortieth stage production.

So great is his passion for the written word, Bradbury says he awakens "each morning with metaphors running through" his head.

Although he never attended college, Bradbury evidenced a deep love of learning. "I went to the library," he says. And there he devoured books on a wide variety of subjects. Today, he is a world-renown author of science fiction novels and plays.

What sets your soul afire? What's your passion?

To each is given the manifestation of the Spirit for the common good. (1 Corinthians 12:7)

Holy Spirit, infuse us with a passion for learning.

Group Therapy

At first, Monica found physical therapy a daunting, difficult task. How would she ever get back to feeling whole again after surgery? But after a few sessions, Monica had a breakthrough—she discovered she wasn't alone.

She started seeing the same people each time she went to the rehabilitation center—and they started to share stories of their own struggles on the road to recovery. They encouraged one another. They shared solutions to common issues.

Above all, for Monica, there was just the joy of having others there as, together, all worked their way back to being physically whole.

Life's struggles—just as its joys—are best when shared.

Two are better than one, because they have a good reward for their toil. For if they fall, one will lift up the other...if two lie together, they keep warm...two will withstand one. (Ecclesiastes 4:9-10,11,12)

Abba, give us companions as we face today's trials.

Lá Fhéile Pádraig Shona Duit!

Here in English is an excerpt from St. Patrick's beautiful *Lorica* or Breastplate (an ancient sort of armored vest):

"Christ with me, Christ before me,/Christ behind me, Christ within me,/Christ beneath me, Christ above me,/Christ at my right,/Christ at my left,/Christ in the fort,/Christ in the chariot seat,/Christ in the poop [deck],/Christ in the heart of everyone who thinks of me,/Christ in the mouth of everyone who speaks to me,/Christ in every eye that sees me,/Christ in every ear that hears me."

May Jesus, Son of God and Son of Mary and Joseph, be with you at every moment and may He be with all those whom you meet today!

Lá Fhéile Pádraig Shona Duit! Happy St. Patrick's Day to you!

A bishop, as God's steward, must be blameless... not...arrogant or quick-tempered or addicted to wine or violent or greedy...but...hospitable, a lover of goodness, prudent, upright, devout, and self-controlled. (Titus 1:7,8)

Triune God, protect our faith and hope in You.

Best Friends Forever

Mel Simmons and Pauline Alighieri were friends for more than 35 years. They met when they were flight attendants based at Boston's Logan Airport. Their friendship deepened with time.

When Simmons was diagnosed with breast cancer in 2000 Alighieri was there for her along with many others who loved Mel Simmons and valued her bright, happy personality. When she died in 2005, Pauline Alighieri started a group called Friends of Mel Foundation in Hingham, Massachusetts, to fund cancer research and to offer helpful, comforting support to those with the disease.

"Our goal is to get them over that hump while they're in treatment," she says. "The kind of thing a friend does when the chips are down." Friends of Mel has sold bracelets and held other fundraisers, collecting more than $4 million dollars.

It's amazing just how much a friend can accomplish.

A friend loves at all times. (Proverbs 17:17)

Jesus, Friend of my soul, how can I best help friends, and strangers, in need?

Prayers-to-Go

Ministry, it seems, can take place anywhere. In Kansas City, Missouri, for example, one parish has discovered that a city bus stop is an ideal place to talk to others about God.

St. James Parish is located just a block-and-a-half from a major bus stop and transfer point. In 2007, the church held a children's drawing contest to see who could create a winning Christmas card design. In the winning entry, a young participant drew a picture of the Holy Family waiting at a bus stop. That image started parish administrators thinking about hospitality, says one church leader, and soon after, St. James' Bus Stop Ministry was born.

The ministry brings snacks, drinks and information about the Church's charitable services to those waiting for a bus. "It's a ministry of hospitality," says one volunteer. "We aim to bring care and concern to persons who ride the bus."

Proclaim the good news, 'The kingdom of heaven has come near'. (Matthew 10:7)

Holy Spirit, how can we comfort those who are far from home?

Just Go For It!

Nancy Andrews was in high school when she first became interested in science. At Yale University, she figured she'd become a scientist or a professor.

As she pursued both a Ph.D. and a medical degree, it never occurred to her that few women pursued careers in research and academic leadership in the late 1970s.

Dr. Andrews also paid little, if any, heed to negative comments and so-called advice as to what she *couldn't* accomplish in her career. She just kept following her heart, and pursued career goals that appealed to her. Ultimately, she became dean of Duke University Medical School.

"If there are unwritten rules that don't make sense to me, I challenge them and see if I can change them," she says.

What senseless unwritten rules in your life need breaking?

I commend to you our sister Phoebe, a deacon of the church at Cenchreae. ...Mary, who has worked very hard among you...and Junia...prominent among the apostles. (Romans 16:1, 6,7))

Father God, instill in Your people the courage to work for equal opportunities for all in all areas of life.

The Grace of Courtesy

Many people don't appreciate the potential power of an act of courtesy, but religious and civil rights leader Desmond Tutu does because such a gesture changed his life.

As a boy, he saw firsthand the evils of South Africa's apartheid system. Injustice and indignities were the norm. One day, as young Tutu walked down the street with his mother, a white Anglican priest politely stepped aside and tipped his hat to her. Surprised, the youngster asked her, "Why was that white man so nice to you?"

She replied, "That man is a minister of the Gospel. People like that are courteous to everyone."

Desmond Tutu later said that he decided at that moment to become a minister of the Gospel. He was eventually ordained an Anglican priest; later, an Archbishop. He won renown as a human rights advocate, winning the 1984 Nobel Peace Prize.

Be courteous and kind!

Show every courtesy to everyone. (Titus 3:2)

Holy Trinity, show me how to express my love and respect for others through my smallest actions.

Cupcakes for Cattle!

Fourth and fifth graders at St. Francis of Assisi School in Warwick, Rhode Island, read "Beatrice's Goat." It's the real-life story of Ugandan Beatrice Biira and the nanny goat, Migisa (Blessing), that Biira and her family received from the Arkansas-based Heifer International. The students learned to help other families in need; the importance of farm animals to indigent families; and that one animal can give so much.

The students decided to hold fundraisers including a school-wide dress down day so that livestock could be bought for families in need. They made $400. Then they baked or purchased cupcakes, many decorated with animal crackers, for sale at lunchtime. They raised an additional $110.

That money was sent to Heifer International to buy livestock and training in animal husbandry for poor families in the U.S. and abroad.

Teach children to share and to care and you will help build a more just world.

Train children in the right way. (Proverbs 22:6)

Inspire parents and educators to teach their children whole-souled, practical generosity, loving God.

Eccentric, and Proud of It

Human beings are indeed resilient creatures! Take Vermont's river towns for example. They have been known as upstart, rebellious and eccentric communities. In a 1937 guide, a Dr. Robert Wesselhoeft of Brattleboro is noted as establishing a mineral spring that attracted Stonewall Jackson and Harriet Beecher Stowe, among others.

In Bellows Falls, Henrietta Howland Robinson Green, then considered the richest American woman, was so miserly that she rebuffed heat, hot water and medical care, even for her own son.

"There has always been real creativity and eccentricity, along with independent thought, here in Vermont," explains Dona Brown, a University of Vermont history professor.

Today, faced with shrinking populations and factory shutdowns, health resorts, natural healing centers and performing arts centers are again springing up among Vermont's river towns.

How quickly do you rebound from life's trials?

The sufferings of this present time are not worth comparing with the glory about to be revealed. (Romans 8:18)

Hold my hand as I walk through life's trials, Jesus.

Placing an Order for Service

You might think it's impressive enough to be the oldest working union waiter in the United States. However, Harold "Billy" DeLong, an 87-year-old from Queens, New York, works 50 to 75 banquets a year, not to support himself, but to support his humanitarian endeavors.

He's assisted victims of Hurricane Katrina and traveled to India, Africa and Vietnam to help poor people there. And he's done all this since retiring from a long career that included military intelligence work. His volunteer efforts have earned DeLong the distinction of being named traveling ambassador for New York's Rotary Club.

"My motto is, 'service above self'," says Delong. "No matter how old you are, you can get out and help others."

Every single one of us can use our talents and ingenuity to help others—if we just make the decision to do it.

To each is given the manifestation of the Spirit for the common good. (1 Corinthians 12:7)

Merciful Savior, show me how to look after others' needs by using the gifts You've entrusted to me.

From a Note on a Candy Bar

As a high school senior in 1953, Ohio resident Betty Dunn sent candy bars to students in Germany and England. It was a goodwill effort organized by her local youth organization. Dunn decided to tape her name and address to one of the bars.

A year later, she received a letter from someone named Heinke in Germany, asking if the two could be pen pals. Heinke had gotten Dunn's "addressed" candy bar.

Some 40 years of correspondence followed. Eventually the women met in Germany. Then within months of her second trip to Germany in 1993, Dunn received news of Heinke's death. Sad at the news, she was still grateful for the friendship they had shared—all because of a note on a candy bar so many years before.

Reaching out to others brings us joy; enriches our lives.

Faithful friends are a sturdy shelter: whoever finds one has found a treasure. (Sirach 6:14)

Thank you, Father, for my friends.

Helping the Needy, One Bowl at a Time

A West Virginia charitable organization has put a new twist on an old tradition. While many organizations help nourish the hungry by hosting meals, or soup kitchens, the Huntington Area Food Bank instead holds an annual "Empty Bowl Fundraiser."

The event works like this: local restaurants donate food which approximates the meals people receive daily at soup kitchens across the country. These establishments delight in supporting this event, one area eatery donated more than 90 gallons of soup one year, says the charity's director. And patrons donate some money for the meal and receive ceramic bowls, crafted by students, teachers and others, as a token of appreciation for their generosity.

Last year, the Huntington Area Food Bank raised more than $10,000 to feed the hungry, which shows that a little creativity goes a long way. How could you pique others' interest in helping the needy?

Hear this, you that trample on the needy, and bring to ruin the poor...the Lord has sworn... I will never forget any of their deeds. (Amos 8:4,7)

Lord Jesus, guide our efforts to change unjust economic policies and structures.

A List to Live By

It started with one e-mail!

Brenda Prohaska of City Island, New York, jotted down some 20 suggestions on building up community—ways to be good neighbors. She then e-mailed her list to a few friends.

Among the actions she advocated: "Share what you have." "Fix it even if you didn't break it." "Greet people." "Buy from local merchants."

Soon the recipients of her communication started replying, sending other ideas, such as: "Hire young people for odd jobs." "Talk to the mail carrier." "Seek to understand." "Learn from new and uncomfortable angles." "Mediate a conflict."

The e-mail correspondence continued for a few days, ending with triple the ideas of the original list.

Facing life's challenges and problems alone can make us feel overwhelmed. But with the help and love of those around us, life's journey gets a little easier.

God so loved the world that He gave His only Son, so that everyone who believes in Him may not perish but may have eternal life. (John 3:16)

Help me, Holy Trinity, to reflect Your love.

The Beauty of Creation and Creator

Do science and faith have to be in conflict?

The answer is a resounding, "No!" according to Dr. Francis Collins, scientist, physician and head of the Human Genome Project. In *Guideposts* magazine, he recounted how a dying patient who asked him what he believed ultimately led Dr. Collins to a life of faith.

"It's true that science has shown us how marvelously complex our bodies and brains are," Dr. Collins says. "And it's true that the hardware for all that complexity was made possible by genetics. But that isn't the whole story. Scientific processes were God's plan to prepare a flesh-and-blood home for the spirit to dwell in. He shaped us over millennia, then gave us each a soul and the desire to be with Him. Science doesn't refute God. It affirms Him, and gives us new respect for the beauty of creation."

Knowledge and faith are gifts from God. Respect them.

From the greatness and beauty of created things comes a corresponding perception of their Creator. (Wisdom 13:5)

Grant me the ability to grow in knowledge and faith each day of my life, Spirit of God.

A Hug Fix

Dee's life seemed to be crumbling around her. After 35 years and two children, her marriage was over. While she battled through a messy, nasty divorce, Dee faced also the death of a beloved aunt who had been a second mother to her. And then, when the divorce was final, her youngest child, who had two children of her own, was diagnosed with cancer.

Dee struggled to be there for her daughter, but, she confessed to co-workers one afternoon, "Sometimes I just need a hug." Maggie immediately stepped up and gave her one. In fact, she told Dee to stop by her office daily for just such an embrace—and even gave her three on Fridays to last through the weekend.

Paying attention and responding to the needs of others works miracles of healing—and hope.

Thus says the Lord...as a mother comforts her child, so I will comfort you. (Isaiah 66:12,13)

Lord, I turn to you in my suffering, knowing You will either heal me or help me to bear it.

Meager Food Supply Just isn't Kosher

Each year, the Metropolitan Council of Jewish Poverty prepares 50,000 bundles of kosher food for Passover to help needy Jews.

In 2008, however, a crippled economy and distressed manufacturers, wholesalers and the government meant fewer donations. The sharp decline in donations was especially difficult for the Metropolitan Council. Typically, 75 percent of food supplies from government programs aren't kosher and do not meet Jewish dietary laws, or *kashrut,* and "kosher meat and poultry is simply not available." So, according to the Council's Chief Operating Officer, Peter Brest, the Metropolitan Council relies on "canned tuna to provide healthy protein to low-income clients."

Whether you're keeping *kashrut* or *halal;* observing Ramadan; or Orthodox Christianity's Great Lent; abstaining on Lenten Fridays; or following other prescriptions of your faith, ask yourself if you view it as an opportunity to worship or a burden to be endured?

The law of the Lord is perfect...sure...right... clear...pure...true and righteous...(better) than... fine gold; sweeter also than honey. (Psalm 19:7,8,9,10)

God, help me walk in the way of Your precepts.

Providing Care for Abandoned Animals

In the usual beauty salon you hear the latest gossip, updates on the kids, real estate, and... animal rescuing? Meet Grato Longoria, hair colorist and animal rescuer. This hip New York colorist has been saving strays for over 21 years.

When he finds abandoned dogs or cats he makes sure they are treated by a veterinarian, and then he either takes them home or finds a friend who will temporarily foster them. No matter what, they will have a safe place to live because Longoria assesses the owner and their home before giving any animal to them. He estimates that he's placed hundreds of animals over the years.

There are many ways to help abandoned companion animals. Contribute your time or money to an animal hospital. Support your local society for the prevention of cruelty to animals. Foster strays. Adopt shelter animals, especially elderly or sick ones. Remember, all life, animal and human, is precious.

Anyone who kills an animal shall make restitution for it. (Leviticus 24:18)

Creator, remind us to express our gratitude for the companionship of dogs, cats and other creatures in the way we care for them.

A Daily Prayer

Prayer can be a formal going apart or a distracted chatting with your dearest Friend, God. Here's an excerpt from a prayer that may help you chat with God as your day begins:

"Dear Lord, I thank You for this day...for my being able to see and to hear.

"Please keep me safe from all danger and harm. Help me to start this day with a new attitude and plenty of gratitude.

"Clear my mind so that I can hear from You. Please broaden my mind.

"Let me not whine and whimper over things I have no control over.

"Bless me that I may be a blessing....Keep me strong that I may help the weak....Keep me uplifted that I may have words of encouragement for others."

"Blessed are You, merciful God! Blessed is Your name forever; let all Your works praise You forever." (Tobit 3:11)

God, inspire me to talk with You at least each morning.

Another Ten Commandments

Here are ten commandments for a more wholesome life:

I. Thou shall not worry. It's unproductive.

II. Thou shall not be fearful. Most things we fear never happen.

III. Thou shall not cross bridges before you come to them.

IV. Thou shall only handle one problem at a time.

V. Thou shall not take problems to bed. They make poor bedfellows.

VI. Thou shall not borrow other people's problems.

VII. Thou shall not try to relive yesterday. Focus on what is happening and be happy now!

VIII. Thou shall be a good listener because some people do know more than you do.

IX. Thou shall not become bogged down by frustration, for 90 percent is rooted in self-pity.

X. Thou shall count thy blessings including the small ones.

Cast your burden on the Lord, and He will sustain you. (Psalm 55:22)

Lord, bless me with your strength and courage.

To Resent and to Forgive

It's been said that bearing resentment against someone is like swallowing poison and expecting that person to die.

It can be hard to let go of anger and antipathy when we've been wronged or hurt. The cause may be great or small, yet we can still become so consumed that we can't see straight. But there is a way out, even if it sounds impossible. It's called forgiveness.

How can we forgive another person who has hurt us or a loved one? We pray in the *Our Father,* "forgive us our trespasses as we forgive those who trespass against us"—but do we mean it?

Forgiveness is both a determined choice and a deliberate act. When we forgive others, we don't just free the other person, we free ourselves. If revenge seems to "even the score," forgiveness does far more. Forgiveness wins the game.

If you forgive others...your heavenly Father will also forgive you; but if you do not forgive others, neither will your Father forgive your trespasses. (Matthew 6:14-15)

Redeemer, forgive my sins and show me how to forgive others.

Thanks Again

What was your earliest lesson in courtesy? Most people would probably say that their parents' nudges ("What do you say to your aunt for the nice birthday gift?") to thank others would be at the top of the list.

"Thank you" remains an essential part of society's give and take. Can the same be said of our conversations with God? Do we regularly express our gratitude to the Source of life and love?

Here are prayers of appreciation worth saying:

- "Thanks and thanks again, O Father, for having granted my petitions and that which I never realized I needed or petitioned." — St. Catherine of Siena

- "Because Thine only Son once sacrificed life's loveliness for me, I thank Thee, God, that I have lived." — Elizabeth, Countess of Craven

- "O God, you have given so much to me; give me one thing more, a grateful heart." — Rev. George Herbert

Cultivate a grateful heart.

O give thanks to the Lord, for He is good; for His steadfast love endures forever. (Psalm 107:1)

Thank You, Loving Lord, not only for all You do for me, but for all You are.

Preaching Where the People Are

Father Robert Lubic of Perryopolis, Pennsylvania, is an inspired preacher. But that's not what's gotten him worldwide attention.

It's his website called thepunkpriest.com that's opened a ministry to those who might otherwise never get in touch with a priest. He says, "I think there are many people who, for whatever reason, have difficulty approaching priests, and because I don't fit any stereotypes, they may feel comfortable with me. In that way, I'm able to reach a lot of people who are marginalized."

His website not only includes a rock version of the song "Here I Am, Lord," but also solemn chants. He uses music to make spiritual points. Father Lubic says, "I've been able to find homily material in a wide range of popular songs, though I often give an entirely different spin than what was originally intended."

Each of us can spread God's love in our own unique way.

Love the Lord your God with all your heart...soul, and...mind...love your neighbor as yourself. On these two commandments hang all the law and the prophets. (Matthew 22:37,39-40)

Let my voice be Your voice, Merciful God, in speaking to my brothers and sisters, whoever and wherever they are.

A Meal for the Mind

You'd never guess Marnita Schroedl's modest Minneapolis home is a center for change.

Yet Schroedl is the founder of Marnita's Table, an ongoing experiment in fellowship and cross-cultural/racial communication over food. Friends, neighbors, activists and concerned citizens regularly gather over a home cooked meal to discuss topics they've suggested; AIDS, discrimination, peace, injustice, among others.

The project was born of Schroedl's experience as the child of an African-American-Latino father and a Danish-Jewish mother who had been adopted by a white couple. Early in life she learned that acceptance was difficult because of her color. In fact, neighbors decided at a town meeting that they "didn't want those people (of mixed or non-Caucasian descent) in (their) town." "I'd never felt welcomed anywhere, so I was always going to make room at my own table," says Schroedl.

Have you and your family extended a welcoming hand to recent transplants in your area?

No longer pass judgment on one another, but resolve instead never to put a stumbling block in the way of another. (Romans 14:13)

Jesus, teach us to accept one another.

A Creed for Life

Basketball Hall of Fame member (as both player and coach) John Robert Wooden's father, Joshua Hugh Wooden, gave him a Seven Point Creed when he graduated from elementary school. It served him well and is well worth considering. Here it is:

1. Be true to yourself.

2. Make each day your masterpiece.

3. Help others.

4. Drink deeply from good books, especially the Bible.

5. Make friendship a fine art.

6. Build a shelter against a rainy day.

7. Pray for guidance and give thanks for your blessings everyday.

You are unique. Cultivate your self. Make the most of it.

Lord, be gracious to us; we wait for You. Be our... salvation in the time of trouble. (Isaiah 33:2)

For the wonders of my being, Creator, be praised!

Shelter Brings Healing Inside and Out

Unfortunately, many homeless shelters don't do much besides housing the homeless. Crowded, noisy, and even unsafe, too many shelters lack truly livable conditions.

The Crossroads Facility in Oakland, California, is trying to change that. Designed to accommodate about 125 residents, the facility may be the only purpose-built "green" homeless shelter. It has a solar-paneled roof, efficient heating, attractive but practical ceiling fans, and windows that can be opened to let in fresh air. Non-toxic paint was used throughout.

Resident Paul McClendon is delighted at the prospect of this new facility. "It's going to be a beautiful place," says McClendon, who was used to the old shelter's leaky ceilings, dangerous electrical shorts, inadequate heating, and dirty couches.

The poor are subjected to indignities the rest of us would never tolerate. How can you restore dignity to the poor?

I was a stranger and you welcomed me, I was naked and you gave me clothing, I was sick and you took care of me, I was in prison and you visited me. (Matthew 25:35-36)

Remind us, Lamb of God, to respect our poor and sick neighbors as though they were You.

The Farmer Finds a Way

Rick Bernstein, a Baltimore investment analyst, loved gardening more than almost anything. He also knew he wanted to do something more with his life.

He started giving produce to local food banks around the time he started reading the Bible and considering his spirituality more seriously. One day, Bernstein said to his wife Carol, "We're not doing enough. I'm wondering if we should take our savings and buy a small farm."

She thought about it and responded, "If you really believe this is a call from God, I'm in."

They bought a 42-acre farm and, with the help of volunteers, turned it into a non-profit program. Bernstein kept his bank job, but works as a farmer after hours. First Fruits Farm has given away millions of pounds of fruits and vegetables to food banks and soup kitchens.

Be willing to open yourself to God's plan for you.

**A generous person will be enriched.
(Proverbs 11:25)**

Jesus of Nazareth, show us how to work not only for our own benefit, but for that of others.

Rising to Her Challenge

At a gathering held to pay tribute to her, tears and laughter flowed as fellow members of the Oakdale Covenant Church recalled Delories Williams' tireless commitment to a mission from her pastor. Thirty years before, her pastor had challenged her to get all of the church's children into college.

The odds seemed overwhelming: the predominantly African-American Chicago neighborhood was poor. Residents had few job prospects. Schools were under-funded and struggling.

But Williams mentored neighborhood kids, arranged academic tutoring, and served as a Girl Scout leader. When students needed help filling out admission forms, she was there. If a child needed a second chance, Williams made sure he or she got that chance.

Williams let nothing stand in the way of her goal, not even cancer. How do you overcome obstacles when pursuing a goal?

Do not show partiality...or deference...Fight to the death for truth, and the Lord God will fight for you. (Sirach 4:22,28)

May I never get discouraged in the struggle for justice, Prince of Peace.

Hurtful Words and Phrases

Bill Bonner was asked, "Who did you used to be?" Police psychologist Ellen Kirschman says people call her "young lady."

Physicians ask, "Did you understand what I told you?" or "You don't want to upset your family, do you?"

Nurse gerontologist Kristine Williams found that demeaning terms or questions addressed to people with dementia caused aggression, depression and withdrawal. Williams says such words say that older adults are incompetent.

Dr. Becca Levy, a psychologist, believes addressing older people in a loud voice or calling an older person "dear" or "sweetie" come from negative images of older men and women as forgetful, feeble and useless.

Age discrimination and negative attitudes toward older adults are common. How can you light one candle of respect for older people? Begin with the words and attitudes with which you speak to them.

Remember your creator in the days of your youth, before the days of trouble come, and the years...when you will say, "I have no pleasure in them." (Ecclesiastes 12:1)

Ancient of Days, remind us to speak to everyone as though speaking to You.

Making Another's Problem Her Own

Los Angeles real estate developer Georgina Miranda was skimming through *Glamour* magazine when she read an article about the brutal rapes of women and girls in the Congo's ongoing civil war. "I couldn't believe this crisis had been going on for so long and I wanted to help," Miranda says.

She decided to climb the world's eight highest mountains in an effort to raise $2.2 million. Her sponsors pledged $50 for every meter climbed. Through the International Medical Corps, this money will provide lifesaving care to the women and girls of Congo and Uganda.

Though Miranda wasn't a great athlete growing up, ongoing violent crimes encouraged her to push beyond her limits to offer at least a partial solution.

What problem halfway around the world or one nearby needs your attention? Don't turn your back on the needs of others.

Give, and it will be given to you. (Luke 6:38)

Gentle Master, help me make my world the better for my being in it.

Keeping the Dream Alive

Andrea Drummond proudly watches her daughter Nia, 14, playing keyboards and singing in a rich, powerful voice. "She's so talented," Drummond observes, adding that Nia has performed with Elton John, Bette Midler and Alicia Keys as a member of the Grammy Award-winning Brooklyn Youth Chorus.

Yet Drummond worries about her daughter's future. They live in Crown Heights, one of New York's roughest neighborhoods. When Nia was bullied at a public school, Drummond transferred her daughter to a private school, where she discovered her talent for music. Unfortunately, tuition payments along with food and rent are hard to meet.

Drummond contacted the employee assistance division at her job and grants helped keep her daughter enrolled and her dreams alive. Says Nia, "I have something to offer in life."

Each of us has something worthwhile to offer the world. Find your gift. Help others find theirs. Light up the world.

You are the light of the world. ...let your light shine before others. (Matthew 5:14,16)

Remind me, Jesus, to shine my little light for the sake of others.

Monks and NASCAR

What does Belmont Abbey College have in common with NASCAR? Answer: a program in motorsports management.

Other colleges have similar courses, but most relate to engineering. The program at this North Carolina college helps broaden the market for NASCAR and other motorsports industries when looking for business leadership.

This Catholic college hopes to add an edge to the education it offers. "We can bring ethics, morals and values of what it means to deal with a whole person, the idea that sports should be a means of developing virtue," says Belmont president William Thierfelder. "I'm hoping we bring that important extra to the process and the program."

Winning the race is important, but it's better to keep life moving on the right track.

Teach me Your way, O Lord. (Psalm 27:11)

Guide me, Holy Spirit. Keep me ever faithful.

Go Ahead, Waste Time!

You're probably used to rushing through your day, though studies show that being harried isn't healthy. According to Dr. Michaela Axt-Gadermann, co-author of *The Joy of Laziness*, moving at a frantic pace elevates levels of stress hormones, which drain energy and make us more susceptible to illness.

Try some of these techniques to slow your life down:

Say "no"! Eliminate causes and commitments that leave you overscheduled and overwhelmed.

Transform endless "to dos" into manageable "must dos." Focus on a short list of what needs to be done today.

Take a time out. Breaks turn down your stress.

Unplug. Several times a day, turn off all the technology to relax, reflect and recharge.

Schedule time to be with the Master of time.

Life is for more than doing. Life is also for just being.

Be on your guard against all kinds of greed; for one's life does not consist in the abundance of possessions. (Luke 12:15)

With every breath, may I praise You, Father.

A Silver Lining in a Dark Cloud

The 2007 shootings at Virginia Tech brought suffering to many families. But Bryan and Renee Cloyd found a constructive way to remember their daughter, Austin.

After the massacre, the couple asked for contributions in honor of Austin to a program that repairs rundown Appalachian houses. The response was amazing.

Bryan Cloyd, a professor at Virginia Tech, offers a class where students spend one weekend working with the house-repair project and the rest of the semester creating other services. The positive effect this had on campus encouraged the university to create, "V.T.-Engage," a program that asks students, staff and faculty to each perform 10 hours of service for a total of 300,000 hours, in honor of those who were killed.

By helping those in need, we can fulfill our own needs.

Give relief to the afflicted. (2 Thessalonians 1:7)

Help the grieving find solace in helping the poor and needy, Merciful Savior.

More From Ben Franklin

It seems as if the inimitable Benjamin Franklin always had just the right advice for any occasion. Franklin offered these tips to help you persuade others to your point of view:

- Be clear in your own mind exactly what you're after.
- Do your homework; be well prepared to answer questions.
- Don't expect to win the first time. Plant the seed and be persistent.
- Learn about the person you're bargaining with and make friends. Present your case in terms of its benefits for them.
- Keep a sense of humor.

If you have good ideas and want to share them, it's worth the time and effort to do your best to share your viewpoint with others.

Pleasant speech increases persuasiveness. (Proverbs 16:21)

When presenting my opinions, Divine Wisdom, help me be persuasive and respectful.

Family Dinner and a Hug

Every Sunday evening, Elliott Glick would gather his family as his small café for dinner. His wife, Monica, would be there, along with his youngest daughter. His oldest son would come as well, bringing along his sons, Jaiden and Ranen.

One Sunday, three-year-old Jaiden stood in the back room of the café after dinner, looking rather sad. His grandmother asked him what was wrong.

"I didn't do anything since I've been here," he told her.

"Oh, but you did," Monica Glick said. "You gave me a big hug right when you came in. All week long, I can think about that and remember that Jaiden loves me."

Jaiden smiled and ran off to tell his dad that he had done something good after all.

Our greatest accomplishments won't make the newspaper, but they will touch the lives and hearts of those around us.

Jesus said, "Let the little children come to Me, and do not stop them; for it is to such as these that the kingdom of heaven belongs." (Matthew 19:14)

Bless those we meet this day, Lord Christ. Help us show them Your love.

New Ways to Recycle and Reuse

Americans annually discard millions of tons of trash. But people who care about their environment need opportunities to recycle and reuse no longer needed items.

Diane Benson Harrington writes in *Women's Day* magazine that giving to Goodwill, for example, is great but also suggests Habitat for Humanity, for example, which might accept unwanted doors, windows or other building supplies.

Organizations that take non cash items are listed at charitynavigator.org and easterseals.com; check the St. Vincent DePaul Society at svdpusa.org to see if there is a local branch that will pick up your donations.

If you have electronics such as cell phones, computers and printers to donate, check out earth911.org, usedcomputer.com, as well as the website of the Environmental Protection Agency.

Your trash might be another's treasure. Share from your surplus.

Give some of your food to the hungry, and some of your clothing to the naked. Give all your surplus as alms. (Tobit 4:16)

Redeemer, help us simplify our living and our lives.

A Gift of Ourselves

Most of us think that we treat others with courtesy and respect. But there are some people who don't wait for others but extend themselves time after time.

One man in his seventies, who visited the hospital emergency room after experiencing severe pain, was admitted for several days' observation. While he was there, he spoke with doctors, nurses, other patients and visitors with kindness, interest and good humor. He welcomed the man who cleaned his room and thanked the woman who delivered his meal trays. He shook hands with the interns who checked on him and even let a medical student practice drawing his blood.

Although he occasionally got impatient or out-of-sorts, he still made an effort to see the people around him as the unique individuals they are.

Appreciate the men, women and young people in your life—and let them know that you do.

The commandments...are summed up in this word, "Love your neighbor as yourself." Love does no wrong to a neighbor; therefore, love is the fulfilling of the law. (Romans 13:9-10)

Use me, Holy Trinity, to carry Your blessings to each person I meet each day.

Border Crossings

Most know her as Reverend Mary, a title that belies the incredibly diverse role the Rev. Canon Mary Moreno Richardson plays in advising Mexican citizens who want to emigrate to the United States.

Richardson, who is Canon for Hispanic ministry at St. Paul's Episcopal Cathedral in San Diego, offers counsel to families on both sides of the Mexican/U.S. border. She explains the dangers and she notes sources of support for those who risk traveling north for work. Her ministry has also brought Canon Richardson face-to-face with the breakdown of communities left behind as villages empty due to northward migration.

Canon Richardson says, "My prayer is that people are able to understand the suffering these immigrants face."

You shall not oppress the alien. ...You shall love the alien as yourself, for you were aliens in... Egypt. (Leviticus 19:33,34)

Remind as we seek justice and mercy, us that we are immigrants or the descendents of immigrants, Father of all people.

On Earth Day

Earth Day was first proposed by the then U. S. Senator from Wisconsin Gaylord Nelson in 1962. On Earth Day, 1970, 20 million Americans, rich and poor, Democrats and Republicans, urban and rural, marched for a sustainable, healthy environment.

Over the years, interest in Earth Day has continued to grow. Here are some ideas for celebrating the day:

Serve and/or eat locally produced vegan/vegetarian meals. Let family and friends know that you're doing this because God is the Creator.

Join an Earth Day event or celebration. Or plan your own. Clean up a public space by yourself or with some friends. Plant a tree. Build a birdhouse.

Begin a Bible study or book group about caring for creation because God cares deeply about His creation. *Serve God, Save the Planet* is one possible resource.

And above all pray for your home, the Earth.

The Lord by wisdom founded the Earth. (Proverbs 3:19)

Creator, how can I live lightly on Your Earth, my home?

These Works of Art are Not for Sale

Observers have said that the handmade, custom guitars that DeeAnn Hendricks creates are not only beautiful, they're gemlike.

In her spare time, Hendricks, a middle-aged grandmother from Excelsior, Minnesota, crafts custom-made acoustic guitars in her basement. A graphic designer by trade, Hendricks taught herself the luthier's craft with a do-it-yourself kit. She has since made 10 acoustic guitars in seven years.

"I just like making something that people are going to enjoy," says Hendricks, who does not sell her creations but rather, gives them away. "You don't put prices on your children," she says, fondly referring to her work-of-art guitars as offspring.

Hendricks herself does not play guitar, but does derive joy from giving to those who do. What can you do to bring joy to the life of another?

A joyful heart is life itself. (Sirach 30:22)

Help me be joyful in all I do, Abba.

Log On to Help

A 125-year-old East Harlem church is getting assistance with its $2 million in needed structural repairs thanks to the Internet.

Former residents of this New York City neighborhood have discussed the problems of Holy Rosary Church and ways to raise money for repairs through a web site that keeps them close to their old home. These parishioners now live in other parts of the city, or as far away as Florida, Virginia and California.

Thomas Saltarelli, whose mother still resides just blocks from the church, began spreading the word online after attending a funeral Mass at the church.

"Growing up, I had always looked at the church as a work of art," he says. "That day, I saw it was in really bad shape." Now, his efforts are bringing in donations to make needed repairs.

When communities gather, in the virtual or real world, prayers are answered and problems solved.

Pray without ceasing. (1 Thessalonians 5:17)

When I call on You, Lord, You answer me, relieving all my fears and insecurities.

Yes, You Are!

Consider the wisdom of the following excerpts from the anonymous poem "I'm Special:"

"There is nobody like me./...my smile...my eyes./...my abilities.

"No one will ever/look, talk, walk or think like me.

"I'm special...rare.

"In all rarity, there is great value.

"God made me special/for a very special purpose.

"A job...that no one else can do.../Only one is qualified...has/what it takes./...me."

There really is no one quite like you. More amazingly, there never will be anyone like you, for all eternity. Use your special gifts to accomplish what no other person can.

Here is My servant, whom I uphold, My chosen, in whom My soul delights...I have called you...I have taken you by the hand and kept you. (Isaiah 42:1,6)

Lord of Lords, remind me that You have a special purpose for my existence, my life.

A Productive Life

Centenarian Ruth Proskauer Smith is an avid supporter of mass transit. Smith prefers buses and subways as her transportation of choice in New York, her home since the early 20th century. "I just get so mad when I'm stuck in traffic and the taxi meter keeps ticking," she says.

While she remembers the New York of the 1910s, these days, she teaches a class on the Supreme Court to retired men and women who participate in a City College educational program.

Aside from her active schedule, she enjoys a freedom only known to those who have lived a century. "I eat what I want," she says, although her penchant for martinis has been curbed in recent years. "I can't do that anymore," she laughs.

Reaching one hundred years of age is not the oddity it used to be. Americans are living longer. What do you plan to do in your 70s? Your 80s? Your 90s? Beyond?

So teach us to count our days that we may gain a wise heart. (Psalm 90:12)

May I treasure each day in Your presence, Jesus Christ.

Cooking Up a Second Chance

On the surface, Culinary Cornerstones, a cooking school rooted in classic French cuisine, looks like any other school for chefs-to-be. During its 12-week program, students wear chef's garb and learn the proper techniques for slicing, dicing and sautéing the finest ingredients.

Yet, it's about far more than cooking. Operated by Episcopal Community Services in Kansas City, the school provides former prison inmates, homeless persons and those suffering from emotional illness a chance at a fresh start.

It's also about redemption, says Rev. Allen Ohlstein, who oversees the program. "Plain and simple, that's the heart of Culinary Cornerstones," he says.

Says one student, "The best thing about this program is the chance to move forward. With our backgrounds, some programs would never let us in. This is the opportunity to change."

When was the last time you were asked to look beyond someone's past mistakes and give him or her a second chance?

Do not judge, and you will not be judged; do not condemn, and you will not be condemned. (Luke 6:37)

Remind us, that You alone are perfect, God.

Follow the Star

Some people who suffer from desperate childhoods manage to create lives of hope, not only for themselves, but for others.

One of them, Harriet Tubman, was born into slavery on a Chesapeake Bay plantation in 1820. She was frequently beaten and was once hit by a weight that left a permanent indentation in her forehead. Finally, guided by the North Star, she escaped to Pennsylvania.

Tubman became a leader of the Underground Railroad. Her many trips bringing slaves North earned her the name, "The Moses of her people." On these dangerous journeys, she encouraged her "passengers," saying, "Children, if you are tired, keep going. If you are hungry, keep going. If you are scared, keep going. If you want a taste of freedom, keep going."

After the Civil War, Harriet Tubman worked for better education and civil rights for former slaves and their children.

Everyone can do good for others if they make that choice.

(The Lord) has sent me to bring good news to the oppressed, to bind up the brokenhearted, to proclaim liberty to the captives, and release to the prisoners. (Isaiah 61:1)

Teach me to follow You, merciful Liberator.

Back on Their Feet

One of the first things Anne Mahlum did when she moved from Bismarck, North Dakota, to Philadelphia, Pennsylvania, was to map out her daily run. She says, "It wouldn't have mattered if I'd moved to Siberia; I have to get my daily run in."

Every day Mahlum would begin her 5 a.m. run past the warehouses, factories and homeless men in her new neighborhood. The men watched her with bewildered interest, and soon asked, "How far are you running today?"

Mahlum felt compelled to share the healing joy she derived from running. She engaged the support of a local mission, and her running group, Back on My Feet, was formed. Today, she leads a group of homeless men on a daily run of at least a mile.

Some of them, inspired by their success at running, have moved out of shelters and gotten paid work. "All things are possible, with the strength we are given," says Mahlum.

There is hope for a tree, if it is cut down, that it will sprout again. ...Though its root grows old... and its stump dies...yet at the scent of water it will bud...like a young plant. (Job 14:7,8,9)

Help me see life's glass as at least half-full, Dear Savior.

Human's Best Friend — For a Day

It's likely that the moniker "man's best friend" was given to dogs because of the companionship, loyalty and love dogs offer their owners.

Now, people who do not own a dog can bask in that canine companionship as needed, while supporting a worthwhile effort to help animal shelter dogs.

Flexpetz rents dogs from shelters to temporary "owners" in the hope that they will eventually be adopted. The company provides day care and boarding for the dogs, which can be "rented" for a day or longer.

Says one doggie renter, "I'm single and a transplant to New York, so when I am walking around with 'Oliver', I am able to meet people more easily."

Dogs, cats and other animals are intelligent, sentient creatures deserving of our respect and care. Support efforts to protect and nurture them while punishing those who abuse them.

Anyone who kills an animal shall make restitution for it, life for life. (Leviticus 24:18)

Endow us with Your own compassion toward all life, human and animal, Creator and Merciful Father.

Not all That Meets the Eye

Drive west along Route 23 south of Columbus, Ohio, past ever larger hills and picturesque Shawnee Hills State Park. The lake there is surrounded by gorgeous flower gardens, affluent properties and walking and nature trails. The impression is that such beauty goes on for miles—but the reality is different.

Just a few miles away, ramshackle trailers, boarded-up homes and abandoned vehicles are the norm. Here is where volunteers from St. Joseph Church work tirelessly to alleviate conditions by planting produce gardens, stocking food pantry shelves and offering other services to struggling families year-round. Donations of all varieties are also collected.

The parishioners see the stark contrast between a wealthy, well-groomed enclave and a poor, struggling community as an opportunity to serve.

How can you do your part to improve even one person's life? What can your parish do to relieve nearby poverty?

**When you give a luncheon or a dinner, do not invite your friends...your relatives or rich neighbors...but...the poor, the crippled, the lame, and the blind. And you will be...repaid.
(Luke 14:12,13-14)**

Remind us, Jesus, that by working for social justice, we are working for peace.

Strategies for Praying Daily

In the Baltimore Catechism, prayer was said to be a lifting up of one's mind and heart to God by setting aside times each day for prayers, often read from a book.

Yet as God's own creatures we need to talk with our Abba and to listen to God daily. Here are suggestions for daily prayer in your words or memorized ones:

- Pray while waiting on line;
- Pray sitting in a doctor's office;
- Pray while waiting for the light to change;
- Pray on the commuter train or bus;
- Pray walking or jogging (Oh the loveliness for which to praise and thank God!);
- Pray for each member of your family as you drift off to sleep - don't worry if you don't finish;
- Pray for different groups or concerns on different days; e.g., the welfare and peace of our Jewish neighbors on Saturdays.

In short P R A Y ! When, where and how you can—in your own words.

Pray without ceasing. (1 Thessalonians 5:16)

Abba, encourage me to talk with You when and where and as I can.

From One Little Swab...

When writer Richard Rubin received a call from a cousin inviting him to a family reunion, Rubin knew he couldn't resist. Rubin had never met this particular cousin. In fact, "I didn't even know he existed before he e-mailed me just days ago," says Rubin. It seems Rubin's cousin had used DNA to trace his lineage.

A few years ago, breakthroughs in genetic testing enabled those seeking information on their ancestry to do so beginning with a simple swab of the cheek. Scientists can spot elements in a person's DNA and literally trace them back to regions of the world where the same, unchangeable genetic elements are found in local populations. As a result, people are making astonishing discoveries about their ancestry:

At the DNA level we are one people. Emphasize what unites us as members of the human race, not our differences.

(Do not) think of yourself more highly than you ought...we are members one of another. (Romans 12:3,5)

Remind us, Creator, of the humanity we share with every other person on this Earth.

Sleeping on Floors, Eating Hot Dogs

A team of men and women ride bikes while wearing matching green, orange, and white shirts. On any other day, they are engineers, teachers, insurance agents, physical therapists. But this day they are part of an advocacy group called Brake the Cycle of Poverty.

These men and women are cycling to raise awareness of poverty and injustice through a series of presentations at Connecticut churches.

The hundreds-of-miles days-long journey includes sleeping on parish hall floors, feasting on hot dogs—and lots of prayer. "When the hills are tough, I say prayers," says cyclist Bob King. "I usually measure hills by how many Hail Marys I say."

Life's journey will surely be filled with tough hills—challenges and sacrifices—but it can also offer the opportunity to do good for others.

Will not God grant justice to His chosen ones who cry to Him day and night? Will He delay long in helping them? (Luke 18:7)

When I am in need, Abba, hear me.

Your Last Chance

Most people would probably say they try to love their neighbors and try to do good for others. But do we really understand the importance and the urgency of fulfilling that ideal?

Rabbi Zelig Pliskin, author of a number of books that encourage readers to lead happy and constructive lives, says, "As an opportunity to do an act of kindness arises, ask yourself, 'If I were going to view this as my final opportunity to do one last good deed in this world, what would I do?' As you contemplate this question, you will experience its amazing power. Because eventually we will be faced with this actual last opportunity. And we never know when it will be."

It's easy to put off little words of kindness or acts of charity, rationalizing that we'll always have tomorrow. But we won't. One day will be our last. What kind of day will it be?

Fear God, and keep His commandments; for that is the whole duty of everyone. For God will bring every deed into judgment, including every secret thing, whether good or evil. (Ecclesiastes 12:13-14)

Holy Spirit, inspire my efforts to lead a good life each and every day You entrust to me.

Flying So Others See

Jim Bevier used to fly packages for FedEx, making sure they arrived overnight. Now retired, this Mississippi native still flies, but it's to make sure that others can see!

Bevier is a volunteer pilot for Orbis, a nonprofit that has fought blindness in developing countries for 25 years. The Flying Eye Hospital that he pilots is a converted aircraft that houses a state-of-the-art ophthalmic surgical and teaching facility.

Landing the large airplane on runways not designed for it is a challenge, but one that Bevier feels compelled to do. "I think of my grand-children back home," he says, "and all I want is for those kids to be able to see their own grandparents for the first time."

What we do for others is sometimes a great gift for ourselves as well.

(Jesus) spat on the ground and made mud with the saliva, and spread the mud on the man's eyes, saying to him, "Go, wash in the pool of Siloam...(He) washed and came back able to see. (John 9:6-7)

Open my eyes that I may see You in others, Jesus.

The Most Precious Gift: Time

Week after week, Dawn Stringfield and her friends gathered in an ecumenical group, seeking to live their faith with courage. After searching their hearts, Lydia's House was born in St. Louis, Missouri.

Lydia's House provides a safe haven for abused women and their children once shelters and other options run out. Battered-women shelters generally provide housing for only 90 days. "There's no way that someone who's been abused can turn her life around in 90 days," says Stringfield. Lydia's House provides 35 women and 70 children with safe housing for up to two years.

For one abuse survivor, the house was a life-changing option. Six years after leaving the center, the woman is working, and in a loving marriage. Says another survivor, "You have to learn that you don't need to prove that you are good enough to be loved."

Support abused women any way you can.

Honor your mother and do not abandon her all the days of her life. (Tobit 4:3)

Holy Spirit, inspire programs to end the abuse of women and children.

Reacting to Nuclear Waste

When Joseph Egan died at the age of 53 from cancer, that wasn't the end of his years-long battle to block a nuclear waste dump at Nevada's Yucca Mountain.

In fact, the obituary published on his law firm's web site said that he had arranged for his ashes to be spread at Yucca Mountain as these words were spoken, "Rad-waste buried here only over my dead body."

His wife, Patricia, told a *New York Times* reporter, "We're going to do it."

Egan's crusade and legal challenges helped set back the Energy Department's project at Yucca. He also filed other related lawsuits, including one to protect workers from illegal waste storage.

All we do and say should reflect our personal standards and beliefs—the values that affirm God's own life within us and within all other people and creatures; and that lead to the common good.

**Be strong and of good courage.
(1 Chronicles 28:20)**

Strengthen me, Lord, that my words and actions be courageous on behalf of others.

From Isolation to Fellowship

The birth of a baby is a time of joy and celebration and, for some moms, isolation, pressure and fear. Caring for a newborn can make connecting with other adults difficult.

So the Mom's Ministry at St. Joan of Arc Church, in Kokomo, Indiana, is reaching out with opportunities to socialize, connect and develop new relationships. Andrea Wyrick, ministry coordinator, says, "We try to help people form relationships." She remembers when only 10 or 12 people were attracted. Membership is now nearly 150.

One member says it's "a great network of people to talk to." Another says she "can get good advice from other moms."

Motherhood involves momentous physical and hormonal changes in a woman; daunting responsibilities. Mothers need all the companionship, love, compassion and help they can get. Reach out to them.

The angel Gabriel was sent by God to...Mary. (When) the angel departed...Mary set out (for)... the house of Zechariah and greeted Elizabeth... Mary remained with her about three months. (Luke 1:26,27,38,39,40,56)

Let us help new mothers, God who blessed Elizabeth and Zechariah in their old age.

Just Write!

The power of the written word has prevailed through the ages. When a thought or fact has been inscribed on clay or written in ink on parchment or paper, it has taken on a life of its own.

E. C. Roy tried for years to develop the discipline of writing regularly in his personal journal. He bought beautiful, leather-bound journals, but once a few pages were filled, he'd stop.

Then, Roy was laid off from his job. The lure of a career as a writer took hold. He says, "My subconscious kept whispering, 'Write, just write'."

Roy made writing each day's first priority. And toward that goal, he decided to write in the morning, when his mind was fresh. It didn't matter what he wrote, just that he wrote something. Soon, dreams, fears, thoughts, uncertainties began to flow onto the pages.

Journaling can offer structure and perspective to your life's events as well as remind you just how unique and special you are.

Thus says...He who formed you...I have called you by name, you are Mine...you are precious in My sight, and honored, and I love you. (Isaiah 43:1,4)

Gracious Lord, thank You for the gift of my unique self.

The School of Loss

Setbacks and disappointments seem a normal part of life. So, is there a way to see the pain as a breakthrough? Perhaps.

Writer Cheryl Richardson credits a friend with helping her see that a painful breakup prepared her for a mature and lasting marriage. She had to "face the fear of living alone." She realized she needed therapy. By growing in self-respect she learned to treat herself better, and to demand that others treat her respectfully, too.

Richardson suggests that in times of disappointments you ask yourself four questions:

1. Which part of me is this loss supposed to strengthen?
2. What can I learn from this?
3. Who can help me transform this loss into gain?
4. How can what I've learned help me help others?

As she writes in *Body + Soul*, "When we get to the other side of a letdown, there awaits a great opportunity to use what we've learned in service to ourselves and others."

Bear fruit with patient endurance. (Luke 8:15)

Merciful Savior, accompany me through setbacks to the fuller, richer life awaiting me.

Caring for God's Good Earth—and Ours

Ever since "going green" gained popularity, people are making better choices on how they treat the earth and themselves. Many are recycling more often and more consciously, but there's more. *Glamour* magazine offers tips to "green-over" your home:

Find new uses for old stuff: "Repurposing things conserves manufacturing energy and landfill space," says Elizabeth Rogers, coauthor of *The Green Book*.

Control temperature with window shades: Raise shades in winter to allow sunlight in; lower them in summer to block it. Reduce both heating and air-conditioning costs.

Use eco-friendly products: paint, towels, sheets, wallpaper or clothes. They help reduce toxins in the air and water.

By practicing these ideas and other "go green" initiatives, you can reduce waste, toxins and chemicals and save fuel and natural resources. How are you going green?

The Lord...formed the earth and made it (He established it; He did not create it a chaos, He formed it to be inhabited!). (Isaiah 45:18)

Creator and Sustainer, inspire our efforts to respect the work of Your hands, the Earth.

A Saint in the Family

It's not often that a family can boast a saint as an ancestor, but the Magallanes family has Cristobal Magallanes, a 20th century Mexican priest-martyr who is a canonized Catholic saint.

St. Cristobal was among those persecuted by the Mexican government of President Plutarco Elias Calles from 1924 to 1928.

St. Cristobal ministered largely in secret. As enforcement of anti-Catholic laws intensified, many Catholics rebelled. St. Cristobal counseled his parishioners to shun violence and armed rebellion. Despite this, he was captured and executed.

The Magallanes are proud of their ancestor. "Devotion to St. Cristobal is growing year by year in Mexico," says one.

Hatred and prejudice by both religious and secular groups bring tragic results. Fight bias and intolerance. Support freedom of religion; separation of church and state.

Hate evil and love good, and establish justice. (Amos 5:15)

Embolden your people to denounce prejudice and intolerance, Holy Spirit.

Care to Share a Bike?

In 2008, a new program was launched in the District of Columbia which officials say is the first of its kind in the nation. The private venture called SmartBike DC allows people to rent a bicycle with the swipe of a membership card.

Experts and city planners are rallying behind the new service. Says one city policymaker, "Our transit systems are already stressed, and this program will help us reduce congestion and pollution," as well as parking problems.

In addition to these potential benefits, there's the health boost. Cycling is a superb form of aerobic exercise, strengthening the heart and providing beneficial effects to the entire body.

One simple idea can lead to a multitude of rewards. Deploy your creative thinking skills all the time but especially when life throws you a challenge.

The Holy Spirit will teach you. (Luke 12:12)

Invigorate our problem-solving abilities, Paraclete, so we may improve our lives and others'.

Not Your Typical Dream Job

Chances are, if you visit a local kindergarten class on Career Day, you won't hear many five-year olds say they'd love to be an oncology nurse when they grow up. Yet, Gigi Gerlach of West Virginia considers her profession "a dream job;" and "one of the most uplifting jobs in the world."

That's because Gerlach sees her role as an oncology nurse as one of hope, encouragement and compassion. In advising patients diagnosed with cancer, Gerlach says, she wants "to be as much a source of strength and hope" for them "as they often are for me."

Gerlach reminds her patients of the importance of hope and positive thinking, especially in the face of seemingly insurmountable odds. "Cancer teaches everyone that hope is a discipline, not an emotion," she adds.

Caring for suffering, dying patients while offering hope and encouragement to their loved ones embodies compassion. Pray for hospice professionals and all caregivers.

He will gather the lambs in His arms, and carry them in His bosom, and gently lead the mother sheep. (Isaiah 40:11)

Good Shepherd, carry in Your arms those health care professionals who care for hospice patients and their loved ones.

Moms after Graduation

Young people are not the only ones who miss their friends after they graduate from high school and move on to college or jobs.

As Peggy Frezon of Rensselaer, New York, watched her daughter graduate, she realized that she would miss the other mothers with whom she had gotten friendly over the years. Writing in *Guideposts*, Frezon recalls that one of them suggested that the moms meet at her house the next month so that they would not lose touch. It became a regular get-together with the women taking turns at hosting the group.

"It's been more than four years since then—the kids are out of college!—and we still meet," says Frezon. "Our children have left the nest, but we have spun our own web of support."

Everyone needs fellowship for comfort, for friendship, for everyday pleasure. Make a point of enjoying the company of others.

Pleasant speech multiplies friends...Let those who are friendly with you be many...your advisers be one in a thousand. When you gain friends, gain them through testing, and do not trust them hastily. (Sirach 6:5,6-7)

Divine Wisdom, encourage me to rejoice in my day-by-day human connections with my neighbors.

When Life Hits You Hard, Hit Back!

It's a safe bet that today most people feel overstressed. In fact, according to the American Psychological Association, *extreme* stress strikes a third of we Americans regularly in addition to the garden variety stress most of us confront daily.

Here's a plan to de-stress your life:

1. Pinpoint your biggest stressor. "When you have a concrete and specific list of everything that stresses you out life becomes more manageable," says Dr. Claire Wheeler of Portland, Oregon. Use your list to mitigate the worst offenders.

2. Find one way to cut stress. Sometimes, acting affirmatively to cut stress in even a small way can help lighten the load.

3. Prioritize your work. In addition to ranking stressors, rank your to-do list from most to least important. Get comfortable with letting the smaller stuff go.

Sometimes we worry too much about everything. By itemizing problems, each one becomes less imposing.

God, the Lord, is my strength; He makes my feet like the feet of a deer, and makes me tread upon the heights. (Habakkuk 3:19)

Help me rely on You for strength, Jesus.

Putting Faith into Action

St. Mary's School in Clinton, New York, might seem like any other Catholic elementary school, with its religious education classes and emphasis on Christian values. But St. Mary's is unique.

Class size is limited to no more than 15 students offering a nurturing environment through more personalized instruction. Further, St. Mary's has successfully blended high academic standards with a practical approach to Christian values. While 100 per cent of the school's students achieved mastery level on New York State's Fifth Grade Social Studies test scores, the school also stresses ways to "put faith into action." St. Mary's Virtues program, for example, is centered on building such personal characteristics as honesty, humility, patience and kindness while emphasizing community service.

Our values and our beliefs should guide our actions from childhood through adulthood.

If a brother or sister is naked and lacks daily food, and one of you says to them, "... keep warm and eat your fill," and yet you do not supply their bodily needs, what is the good of that? (James 2:15-16)

May my faith be behind all that I do, Adoni.

Saving Sentences

Evangeline Parsons Yazzie, a Navajo professor at Northern Arizona University, has helped state officials in New Mexico become the first to use a Navajo language (Dené) textbook in the public education system.

"Overall, we believe it will help improve academic education," says New Mexico's Education Secretary, Veronica Garcia. Research shows that students who master their native language often more easily understand abstract concepts in English.

Yazzie's text is also helping to preserve the Navajo (Dené) language. Because of its long oral tradition, the language appears to be dying among young people, tribal officials fear. Each chapter begins with a cultural lesson. Yazzie looks forward to students sharing the book with Navajo elders and, she says, "pretty soon conversation will be sparking around fires."

No matter the language we speak, our words, like our actions, should be filled with love and foster hope.

Are not all these...Galileans? And how is it that we hear, each of us, in our own native language...them speaking about God's deeds of power. (Acts 2:7,8,11)

I tell of Your wondrous deeds, Lord, singing Your praises.

Moving Out, Helping Out

College graduation time is one of anxiety, excitement, and lots of unwanted stuff. Students moving out of dorms dump unused and unwanted clothing, canned goods, bikes, cleaning products and toner cartridges, etc. in the garbage. But New York University is making an effort to change that, not just for the environment, but for those in need.

A room is reserved for donations, and students can drop off anything that can be reused, recycled or resold. "Students who aren't even particularly environmentally concerned can reduce their environmental impact without even thinking about it," said student Kate Fritz. Green Apple Move Out collects these unwanted items and nonperishable foods and donates it to homeless services groups. This helps the environment and homeless people.

Your donations and good deeds can help your planet—and the needy!

Greedy injustice withers the soul. (Sirach 14:9)

Inspire young adults to be generous, Jesus.

A Fabric Woven of Tradition

When Braden Brown was baptized, he was keeping a century-old tradition alive. He wore the same baptismal gown as did his great-great grandfather Richard Cole in 1909.

In photos of the two infants, the gown remains remarkably similar. After it was first used in Cole's baptism, the gown was handed down and has been worn by 16 descendants.

The gown is made of broadcloth cotton, with an outer garment of delicate cotton lawn. It's stored in acid-free paper and wrapped in cloth. Because of its fragile nature, it can only be spot-cleaned, and must be quickly packed up after each use.

Using the gown represents more than tradition, it's a sign of love and care. Says one family member, "We think of how Richard's mother, Sarah Cole, would have felt" when she first dressed her son in the gown.

Tradition can be a thread that helps keep a family close. What are your family's traditions?

Ascribe to the Lord, O families of the peoples, ascribe to the Lord glory and strength.
(1 Chronicles 16:28)

Teach me to honor my ancestors by the whole-souled integrity of my life, Abba.

Dogs Definitely Allowed

Honor, Glory and Gem are three dogs who make their rounds each Monday at St. Mary's Hospital in Amsterdam, New York.

The therapy dogs, owned by Debra Middleton, a former hospital technician, visit units at the hospital, including those for mental health and alcohol rehabilitation. Middleton and her canine companions help patients and their families cope with illness and the emotional distress that often accompanies it.

"They are gentle and intelligent," she says of her dogs. "Their very presence in a room draws people to them."

David Pilliod, director of St. Mary's Pastoral Care Center, adds, "When people are with these dogs, touching, petting and praying with them, they seem to open right up, relax and allow the presence of these animals to heal them."

Healing hope can enter our lives when we need it most, though and not always the way we pictured it.

God anointed Jesus of Nazareth with the Holy Spirit and...He went about doing good and healing. (Acts 10:38)

Father, come to me this day with Your healing.

...For the Long Haul

Rev. Ron Rolheiser, OMI, is a columnist with some wise thoughts on "the long haul."

He suggests that we "have an unlisted ideological number" and instead be women and men "of faith and compassion."

That we "stand with the marginalized" even as we "relate warmly and deeply to every kind of person and group."

That we be both pious and iconoclastic; bowing in reverence and smashing false idols.

That we balance intimacy with Jesus and social action, after Dorothy Day's example.

That we be thoroughly rooted in this breath-takingly lovely, yet sometimes ugly, world and thoroughly rooted in the barely glimpsed world to come.

Be women and men of moment-by-moment, whole-souled, deeply honest, communion with God. Moment-by-moment ask for grace for the long haul.

For freedom Christ has set us free. Stand firm and do not submit again to a yoke of slavery. (Galatians 5:1)

Blessed Trinity, give us grace for the now and the long haul.

Angels for the Homeless

When you hear the name Danielle Steel, you think of the popular author of bestselling novels. But Danielle Steel helping the homeless? In fact, the author's been on a secret mission for over a decade; handing out clothes and food late at night in San Francisco.

Steel and her 11-member team called Yo! Angel! have served over 30,000 people. The team drives around with four vanloads of supplies, looking for homeless people. Yo! Angel! provides warm clothes, sleeping bags, bedding, tarps, ponchos and umbrellas, personal-hygiene supplies and packaged food. Steel adds, "We also give them hope that someone cares about them and good things can happen even at the worst of times."

She adds that "Dealing with homeless feels like emptying the ocean with a thimble. But sometimes making a difference in the world happens one person at a time."

Start small, but start today.

**Those who are generous are blessed.
(Proverbs 22:9)**

Merciful God, remind us to work for long term solutions to the homelessness and poverty in our country.

Parents — Life's Talking!

Often the most useful advice on parenting isn't found in books or from experts, but from conversations with family and friends who've been through it all. Consider these lessons learned from raising children.

You can't multi-task parenthood. "My life, like many mothers', is crazy busy," said Alissa Cohen of Scottsdale, Arizona, "but taking the time to stop what you are doing and focus on what your children are saying is invaluable."

There's happiness in unhappiness. A San Francisco parent observes, "Help your children to cope with unpleasantness, and they'll grow up to be happier in the long run."

There's no such thing as 'even-steven'. A big worry in raising children is treating them equally. One grandmother once observed: "You can't even-steven their lives. You need to treat them uniquely, not equally."

The best decision for parents is to love their children, abundantly and unconditionally.

Love is patient...kind....not envious or boastful or arrogant or rude...not irritable or resentful; it does not rejoice in wrongdoing, but rejoices in the truth. (1 Corinthians 13:4-6)

Abba, help me mirror Your love for the children in my life.

The Sweet Smell of Success

Lisa Price has loved fragrances since her childhood. "I used my allowance to buy perfume," she admits. Enamored with the beauty of different fragrances and aromas, Price began to blend her own perfume concoctions, as both a hobby and a way to relax.

At her mother's suggestion, Price tried selling her creations at a local flea market. When she sold out on her first day, Price was hooked. Little by little, her business grew, as she wisely listened and responded to her clients' requests and suggestions. Her product line expanded, and soon, "Carol's Daughter Bath and Body Works" was born.

Price attributes her success to her mother. "As I was growing the business, I would feel overwhelmed," she says. "My mother taught me to smile through adversity. It's appropriate that the company is named after her."

Remember those who nurtured you.

Those who respect their mother...lay up treasure. (Sirach 3:4)

Help me express my gratitude and respect for my parents, my Father and my God.

Our Healthy Minds

Are you healthy? While certain diseases or defects can be hidden, people generally know what kind of shape their bodies are in. But what about their minds? Just what is a healthy mind?

Dr. William Menninger, co-founder of the renowned Menninger Clinic, now located in Houston, Texas, had this to say on the subject: "Let us define mental health as the adjustment of human beings to the world and to each other with a maximum of effectiveness and happiness. Not just efficiency, or just contentment—or the grace of obeying the rules of the game cheerfully. It is all of these together. It is the ability to maintain an even temper, an alert intelligence, socially considerate behavior, and a happy disposition. This, I think is a healthy mind."

If you or a loved one has ongoing problems that interfere with having a healthy and happy mind, don't be afraid to seek professional help.

A heavy yoke is laid on the children of Adam... perplexities and fear...anger and envy...unrest, and fear of death, and fury and strife. And... visions...like one who has escaped from the battlefield. (Sirach 40:1,2,5,6)

Divine Physician, bless and heal my mind, my body, my soul, my whole being. Bless my brothers and sisters, too.

A Slow Path to Recovery

Nancy George of Richardson, Texas, remembers how, at four years old, her "rough-and-tumble, impossible to-keep-up-with" son Andy was the spirit of energy.

When Andy was not quite five years old, however, George learned the unthinkable: her son had leukemia. She wondered, "How can such an active, healthy child be this sick?"

Nearly frozen with fear, George pursued medical help for her young son. The child had to endure painful spinal taps, difficult chemotherapy and countless visits to doctors as well as overnight hospital stays. It seemed endless, and each year, George feared, could be her son's last.

But George never gave up hope, and today, while she remembers those difficult days, gives thanks for the outcome. Andy is a healthy 16-year-old preparing for his future. "Thank you, Lord," she says.

Sometimes, tragedy brings our priorities into sharper focus. What gifts are you taking for granted?

Give thanks to the Lord, for His steadfast love endures forever. (2 Chronicles 20:21)

Thank you, Prince of Peace, for every uneventful day.

Dogs in Jail

William Campbell told the people gathered about the injuries he sustained in the Iraq War and about how grateful he was to them for giving him Pax, his yellow Labrador retriever.

You see, Campbell's audience, 27 women at New York's Bedford Hills Correctional Facility, helped train Pax as part of the Puppies Behind Bars program.

Pax helps Campbell maintain peace of mind, especially when nightmares from combat flood back.

Hearing about what Pax and other dogs have accomplished gives these women a deep satisfaction. Rosalie Cutting, who is serving time for murder and has two grandsons who served in Iraq, trained a dog named Greta to help a blind woman. "We can't change why we're here," she said. "But I changed somebody's life."

Grave errors and small mistakes are part of everyone's life. But nothing should take away our impulse to do good for others.

Do to others as you would have them do to you. (Luke 6:31)

Remind me to treat others justly, Lord. And forgive me the wrong I do today.

Words to Carry With You

Each year, thousands of families celebrate a friend or family member's graduation from high school or college. For them, it's a time of hope, optimism, excitement and trepidation. After all, leaving one phase of life behind and moving into unfamiliar territory can be hard.

Consider the following passages, taken from sermon by a school chaplain at graduation ceremony:

- As Jeremiah reminds us, "The Lord is at my side." Always keep that thought at the center of your life.
- You must respect and forgive yourself. Until you accept and even love your weakness and vulnerability, you will never know the meaning of God's strength.
- Be nobody's victim. Keep your integrity, protect your heart, and learn to say "no."
- Accept the darkness and disappointments in your life. Without some form of suffering, you will never become compassionate.

Beautiful words to live by!

The Lord is with me. (Jeremiah 20:11)

Carry me in Your sheltering arms, close to Your comforting heart, Good Shepherd.

Wounded Veterans Have a Chance to Heal

More than 30,000 U.S. military personnel have been awarded a Purple Heart for combat injuries sustained during the Iraq and Afghanistan conflicts. For many of these, a vacation is the last thing on their minds.

But Vacations for Veterans, a non-profit, is working to change that. It pairs Purple-Heart recipients with homeowners willing to donate a week at their vacation homes.

The response has been overwhelming, says founder Peggy Carr. More than 250 homeowners and 50 veterans participated in the program in its first few months. Lt. Col. Andy Kaufmann and his family spent a week at a New Hampshire getaway thanks to one donor. Kaufmann had been injured in Iraq and is recovering from 7 surgeries in 18 months. Minnesotan John Feldman donated his Florida condo and frequent-flyer miles. "It's the personal connections that mean most to me," he says.

Respect the brave men and women of the U.S. military even as you pray for an end to wars.

Pay to all what is due them...respect to whom respect is due, honor to whom honor is due. (Romans 13:7)

Protect our members of our armed services, Father of all.

Talking Teens to Safety

Teenager Adam Blomberg survived a near fatal car crash. And, as an adult, Dr. Adam Blomberg talks about it every chance he gets. "I'm trying to save lives, one teenager at a time," says the Boston anesthesiologist.

He's created a presentation for high school students illustrating the dangers of behaving irresponsibly in a car, from not buckling up to speeding to driving under the influence of drugs or alcohol. He also tells his own story, and the more tragic one about his stepbrother Michael, who was killed in a car crash at age 22 because he, like Adam, hadn't been wearing a seatbelt.

"I realize that I may not be able to persuade all of you," he tells teens, "but if I can reach just one of you, it's worthwhile."

Each day presents moments to make a difference for at least one person. Keep your eyes open for that opportunity.

Remember your Creator in the days of your youth. (Ecclesiastes 12:1)

Protect me, Lord, when the shadows of this day threaten Your love-filled light.

Getting to Know You...

Few men and women would say they believe that after the wedding a married couple always lives "happily ever after," yet many neglect to prepare for the actual life-long work involved in creating a lasting marriage.

Engaged couples need to recognize that they will be dealing with a vast range of issues, including finances, sexuality, work, leisure, in-laws, religion and communication. They need to be prepared to pursue the truth about each other and themselves.

One man said, "I thought being engaged meant getting to know my future wife. After we were married, I realized I hadn't spent enough time getting to know myself." Real commitment demands understanding yourself and what you want out of life as well as who your future spouse is and what's important to him or her.

Engaged couples should prepare for the marriage of a lifetime more than a wedding.

Love is strong as death, passion fierce as the grave. Its flashes are...a raging flame. Many waters cannot quench love, neither can floods drown it. (Song of Solomon 8:6-7)

Spirit of Love, guide engaged couples in preparing together for their lifetime of companionship and compassion.

Staying Focused

On their first trip up Alaska's Mt. Alice, Stephanie Millane and a friend were enjoying the magnificence of the view. Then her friend fell 75 feet, breaking her leg.

Reaching for her cell phone, Millane found she had no service. "God," she prayed, "take away my panic." In that moment, she focused, recalling what she learned in a wilderness first-aid course she had taken some time before. Millane made her friend comfortable. Then, by walking a short distance, she found cell phone service and called for help. A helicopter eventually arrived to take them to safety.

In the face of danger and difficulties, take a step back. Solutions will come into focus.

Cast all your anxiety on (God), because He cares for you. (1 Peter 5:7)

Help me keep You, my Divine King, at the center of my life.

Not Waiting for the Other Shoe

During the course of a major business convention, two women found everything going smoothly, so much so that it frightened them.

"I don't know about you," said one, "but things just seem to be so right. All our plans are working out, and all we hoped to accomplish is happening."

"I know what you mean," agreed the other. "I find myself sitting here just waiting for the proverbial 'other shoe' to drop."

As they attended an afternoon seminar, the two heard the presenter speak of how plans for a future initiative were moving along even better than expected. "Sometimes the other shoe doesn't drop," he said, randomly using their exact analogy.

The women exchanged glances, convinced in that moment, that they might just be hearing the truth.

In your own life, trust in the goodness of God is sometimes a leap of faith, but hold on to an all-empowering hope.

Those who trust in the Lord...shall be like a tree planted by water, sending out its roots by the stream. It shall not fear when heat comes. (Jeremiah 17:7-8)

Strengthen my faith, Master, that I may always rely on Your goodness.

The High Cost of Poverty

When we think of the disparity between the "haves" and the "have nots" we tend to focus on possessions. But the differences may run far deeper.

A new study of 9- and 10-year-old children shows that some brain functions are at a much lower level among low-income groups than among youngsters from wealthier families. In fact, the variation is almost equivalent to damage from a stroke.

Researchers say that language development and the ability to plan, remember details and pay attention are especially affected. The underlying reasons may range from malnutrition to stress to exposure to lead and other toxins.

Susan Neuman, a professor of education at the University of Michigan, says that children need "incredibly intensive interventions to overcome this kind of difficulty."

Poor children and their parents need all the help we can provide to allow them to do and be the best they can.

'Truly I tell you, just as you did not do it to one...of these, you did not do it to Me'. (Matthew 25:45)

Your children are counting on us, God of all, to help them grow into healthy and productive adults. Guide our efforts.

Words of Grace and Thanks

When you were a child, did you say grace before eating? Many people still do, although, perhaps because we have fewer family meals together, the custom seems to be waning.

Still, whether our words are spontaneous or learned long ago, such as "Bless us, O Lord, and these Your gifts..." there's value in them. It's an opportunity to thank God for His blessings, to recall ourselves to His presence, and to acknowledge our relationship with our brothers and sisters and all creation.

Writer G.K. Chesterton went even further: "You say grace before meals. All right. But I say grace before the concert and the opera...and grace before I open a book, and grace before sketching, painting, swimming, fencing, boxing, walking, dancing, and grace before I dip the pen in the ink."

We might try doing the same by taking a brief time-out for God before our various daily activities.

Seven times a day I praise You for Your righteous ordinances. (Psalm 119:164)

Remind me to recall myself to Your loving presence frequently throughout the day, Heavenly Father.

When Most Would See a Half Empty Glass

First, a 20-year abusive relationship caused her to lose vision in an eye. Then, in 2003, she learned that the same violent partner had infected her with H.I.V.

Still, Patricia Clouden feels no self pity, saying, "I'm a warrior." Clouden is one of many H.I.V. positive women who are over 50 and who have found support, fellowship, and counseling as part of Iris House's Divas program in Harlem.

While it may be hard to believe, women are the new face of AIDS. According to the Centers for Disease Control and Prevention, 27 percent of people with AIDS are women, up from less than 5 per cent twenty years ago.

Despite the gravity of her circumstances, Clouden expresses only hope. "My future is very bright," she insists. "I'm going to see my grandchildren graduate."

It's easy to be positive when things are looking up. The test of character comes in challenging times.

In passing judgment on another you condemn yourself. (Romans 2:1)

Precious Savior, end the bigotry experienced by many HIV/AIDS patients. Guide researchers working for a cure.

Growing Old 101

Legendary actor Kirk Douglas spoke with *Newsweek* magazine about dealing with old age. "One way is to not hesitate to laugh at yourself," he said. "Humor helps longevity."

Seeing depression as the greatest obstacle of old age, Douglas proposes thinking of others and trying to help them. "You will be amazed how that lessens your depression," he says. "That satisfaction is priceless."

Along with his wife Anne, his outreach has recently included helping to build 400 safe playgrounds for the children of Los Angeles, and starting a recovery center for women addicted to alcohol and drugs. He also supports a continuing education program for students who had thought of dropping out of high school, and a theater program to develop the talents of young artists.

No matter our age, our spirits are renewed when we reflect God's love, in word and deed, to those around us.

The Lord God...will gather the lambs in His arms, and carry them in His bosom, and gently lead the mother sheep. (Isaiah 40:10,11)

From the beginning to the end of my days, Loving Lord, hold me in Your strong arms.

The Sensitive Tourist

Next vacation, take photos that are fun, interesting, and culturally relevant. Don't worry about being a skilled professional. Here are Stephanie Glaros suggestions from an article in *Utne Reader:*

Ask questions. Find out from your concierge or knowledgeable local how people generally feel about being photographed.

Go alone. A solo traveler is more likely than a group to be invited into a local's home for a closer look at everyday life.

Learn some phrases. People will appreciate your attempts to communicate with them in their own language. Remember to say, "please," "thank you," and "hello".

Smile. Be friendly.

Be polite and brave. Ask permission before taking someone's photo.

Compose your picture. Make sure your main subject is in focus.

Treasure your memories, as you enjoy today.

The...fool rushes into a house, but an experienced person waits respectfully outside. (Sirach 21:22)

Blessed Trinity, help us take respect-filled delight in the varieties of human culture.

Connecting and Contributing

As volunteers from the Bread of Life Food Drive sorted through 60,000 donations of canned foods, they were accompanied by an inspirational song playing from a nearby stereo, "Cheer, cheer for old Notre Dame, wake up the echoes cheering her name!"

The Notre Dame Club of Staten Island, New York, has organized a food drive for the past 17 years. Each year, club members from diverse career backgrounds: high school students, bankers, lawyers, plumbers, union members, and doctors unite to lend a hand for this good cause. Not all are alumni. Many joined out of fondness for the school and to give assistance in the drive.

"You've got middle-class, rich, union and non-union," said Anthony Scutari, an electrician and non-alumni member, "everybody is just helping each other to help other people."

By joining together, we can create a positive change in our world.

Always seek to do good to one another and to all. (1 Thessalonians 5:15)

The need for nutritious food and potable water is real. But there are many other needs, too. God, remind us to put aside differences and unite to help supply these needs.

And the Band Plays On...

They use a portable stage, and their membership has changed over the years, but the Bath Municipal Band in Brunswick, Maine, continues to play on.

Formed in 1961, the band traces it origins to the early 20th century, when the tradition of playing music at ship launchings, clam festivals and command-changes at military posts was the norm.

The musicians come from all walks of life: students, carpenters, engineers, professors, a doctor, a nurse, and a car dealer among others. Membership has changed over the years, with some joining the ensemble for one performance and others playing with the group for decades. One common thread among them all is that they are volunteers, playing music together to maintain tradition and serve their community.

Locals say the band is a kind of life force. Communities need support to thrive. How can you inject new life into your community?

"For whom am I toiling," (solitary individuals) ask, "and depriving myself of pleasure?"...Two are better than one, because they have a good reward...if they fall, one will lift up the other. (Ecclesiastes 4:8,9,10)

Remind us, Father, that we were not meant to be solitary.

Cultivate Your Marriage

Over busy? Who isn't? Scared by the economic crisis? Sure. But don't let these damage your marriage. Cultivate it instead:

- celebrate a monthly anniversary
- give your spouse the gift of time: reschedule a meeting or forgo a favorite weekend activity to be with him or her instead
- after the kids are in bed, snuggle to music, even briefly
- schedule a mandatory annual weekend getaway
- read to one another
- share memories of one another's childhoods
- snatch moments of time together
- feed the kids early; then the two of you prepare and eat a romantic dinner
- buy tickets to a special favorite event

God gave you to one another. At all times, but especially in difficult times, take refuge in each other's arms.

If I...do not have love, I am a noisy gong or a clanging cymbal...I am nothing...I gain nothing. (1 Corinthians 13:1,2,3)

Wedding Guest at Cana, help spouses cultivate their marriage.

Nurturing Your Soul

Do you enjoy the beauty of a garden? Do you take pleasure in caring for plants and flowers?

Gardening can not only enrich your senses, it can inspire your very soul. That's what Teresa of Avila believed. A mystic, religious reformer, Doctor of the Church and saint, she combined the sacred and the secular in her life, comparing spiritual development with tending a garden.

She wrote: "Beginners must realize that in order to give delight to the Lord they are starting to cultivate a garden on very barren soil, full of weeds. God pulls up weeds and plants good seed. And with the help of God we must work like good gardeners to get these plants to grow and take care to water them so that they don't wither but come to bud and flower. Then God will often come to take pleasure in this garden."

Invite God to help you tend to your soul.

My beloved had a vineyard on a very fertile hill. He dug it and cleared it of stones, and planted it with choice vines. (Isaiah 5:1-2)

God of love and loveliness, transform my soul into a place of beauty where You are always welcome.

Bigger and Better

How important is community? How important is being part of something bigger than you are?

A few years ago at Paul VI High School in Fairfax, Virginia, a class wrote an essay about those questions which is worth sharing: "In America, you are not required to offer food to the hungry or shelter the homeless. There is no ordinance forcing you to visit the lonely, or comfort the infirmed. Nowhere in the Constitution does it say you have to provide clothing to the poor.

"In fact, one of the nicest things about living here in America is that you really don't have to do anything for anybody. But when you do, you give meaning and provide soul to the concept of community and develop a sense of purpose to something greater than one's self."

Each of us needs to value other people as well as ourselves, as individuals and as part of a wider community.

God created humankind...in the likeness of God. Male and female He created them, and He... named them "Humankind." (Genesis 5:1-2)

Loving Lord, help me to reach out to my neighbors, my siblings.

Bikers For Animals

Gruff, beefy and tattooed from head to toe, the bikers of Rescue Ink wear leather, have menacing looks, ride Harley "hogs," and share a passion for caring for homeless, sick and abused animals.

The group was born out of the members' experiences volunteering at animal shelters and the American Society for the Prevention of Cruelty to Animals. These put them in touch with the horrors and abuse that animals suffer from their owners and others.

Rescue Ink was formed to combat animal abuse and neglect in the New York area. They travel to schools to educate children on caring for animals and on having compassion for them. They track down leads in animal abuse and neglect cases, help place abandoned animals in homes, and work closely with suspected abusers to help turn the situation around.

Appearances are usually deceiving. Look beyond the outside to get to know the real inside.

Do not judge by appearances, but judge with right judgment. (John 7:24)

Open my eyes and mind to what's beneath surface appearances. Help me accept all my neighbors, Savior.

Vacation at "Hotel Home"

It was summer in Scottsdale, Arizona, and Jeanne and Louis Hill were going stir crazy. Typically, the retired couple would travel extensively during the Southwest's mercilessly hot summers. This time, Louis's heart condition and medications kept them home.

Rather than gripe, they got creative. "Why not design our own mini-vacation, right here, in Scottsdale?" asked Jeanne.

For the next week, the couple vacationed locally, visiting botanical gardens, museums, theatres, dining out, and enjoying the splendor of the Southwest. "I had no idea this place was so beautiful," said Louis, as they traveled a desert wildflower trail.

By week's end, the couple was refreshed, restored and reconnected in a way that they might have been missed had there been air travel, schedules, and suitcases.

See opportunities in every one of life's challenges. You'd be surprised at how far a little creativity can take you.

Enjoy life with the wife whom you love. (Ecclesiastes 9:9)

God, inspire and strengthen couples as they age.

Families Getting Involved

It's important to get the whole family involved in helping others. This teaches children important lessons for the present and for the future. Some ideas from parents.com:

- Donate clothes. Let children select clothes and/or toys they wish to donate. Go together to the donation site.
- Help elderly neighbors. Rake leaves, wash cars, shovel snow, spread deicer on walks, walk or groom the dog.
- Celebrate birthdays, bas and bat mitzvahs, confirmations, and graduations by suggesting donations to a favorite charity.
- Buy dog or cat food for the humane society and help the children donate it. Let them spend time with the animals.
- At your church or synagogue host the weekly coffee hour, fold the service leaflets or help with maintenance as a family.

Show children by your example that helping others is the only ethical way to live.

Whoever has two coats must share with anyone who has none; and whoever has food must do likewise. (Luke 3:11)

Holy Spirit, teach us from childhood the joy of sharing.

Abilities, Not Limitations

Kyle Kratschman is not an experienced farmer, but in a short time, he learned how to prune damaged leaves from cucumber plants like a seasoned gardener.

Kratschman was born with only 20 percent hearing and later suffered a brain injury. Yet, his work at Cape Abilities has helped him nurture his capabilities rather than the limitations he faces daily.

Cape Abilities is a non-profit organization that provides employment and other services for people with disabilities on Cape Cod, Massachusetts. The 50 employees learn to grow and harvest tomatoes, eggplant, cucumbers, and lettuce, then sell the fresh produce from an on-site stand.

The group's executive director, Larry Thayer, says, "People are looking to be employed in a meaningful way." Because a person faces limitations does not mean that he or she is unable to contribute.

How can you increase opportunities for the disabled in your neighborhood?

Help the weak. (1 Thessalonians 5:14)

Fortify the disabled with perseverance, Lamb of God.

Daughter Teaches Dad

Michael Daley remembers the day his daughter Cara brought home the spring sports sign-up sheet. Immediately, this Cincinnati high school teacher had visions of his six-year-old taking her soccer team to glory.

During one close match, he watched his daughter as she sat on the sidelines, waiting to go into the game. Instead of paying attention to the action on the field, she and her friends were making flower bouquets.

At first taken aback by Cara's actions, Daley soon realized he was the one learning a lesson: winning or losing is never as important as recognizing the joy and beauty that abounds in our lives and the people who are there to share it.

Eat your bread with enjoyment, and drink your wine with a merry heart....Let your garments always be white....Enjoy life with the wife whom you love....Whatever your hand finds to do, do. (Ecclesiastes 9:7,8,9,10)

Help me to treasure time and to praise and thank You, Lord.

Fathers and Sons in Unity

The phrase "like father, like son" is coming to life at a special Eagle Scout project in Indianapolis.

For years, the staff of Our Lady of Fatima Retreat House in Indiana wanted to build a quiet prayer space among the retreat's 13-acres of wooded property. But they didn't have the resources to accomplish it.

Eagle Scout Sam Stapleton and his father, Steve, made the dream a reality. They built a large wooden cross and two wooden benches to create a prayer and meditation space in the woods on the side of the Retreat House entrance.

Says Sam, "The cross was the most personal part of the entire project," he says. "Scouting is about leadership, but I think this project had another dimension. I think about how God will work through the cross when people come to this spot."

The Stapletons' project will help bring peace and spiritual meaning to others' lives. What can you do to bring others peace and spiritual meaning?

Blessed are those who hunger and thirst for righteousness. ...Blessed are the merciful. ...Blessed are the peacemakers. (Matthew 5:6,7,9)

Father, remind us that we each work in Jesus' name.

Love...Bears It Out

When Layng Martine first saw Linda, he decided that if she'd have him, they'd marry. They did marry, settled in Nashville, and raised three sons.

Linda was always athletic, but these days when she does marathons, drives a car, goes up and down hills, it's in a wheelchair. After 15 years of marriage, a car crash made Linda a paraplegic. That doesn't just mean no walking, it means a body that works only from her chest up.

Yet, Martine writes in *The New York Times,* "the hopeless crush I have on her is as wonderfully out of control as when I first saw her. I still get excited when I pull in the driveway and know that I'll see the sexy, beautiful, very funny person I live with. And, later on, snuggle up to her in bed."

Martine adds, "We are two, but we are one. And I love those numbers." Who couldn't admire such whole-souled love?!

**My beloved is mine and I am his.
(Song of Solomon 2:16)**

Incarnate Love, bless couples with love which does not alter, but flourishes and grows.

Helping Kids Grow Well

As a mom of seven children as well as a foster parent, Karen Guidarelli isn't just raising her own children; she's helping others, too.

After moving to Victor, New York, Guidarelli read that half the kids in nearby Rochester didn't graduate from high school and 82 per cent qualified for free lunch. "I had to help," she says.

Buddies, Bridges and Brains was born. With the help of her own teens' fellow high school students, they read to pre-schoolers and gave each a new book and handmade keepsake blanket. The teens also became pen pals, attended community events, and raised money for field trips with the younger children.

The teens benefited, too. Says Guidarelli, "Buddies, Bridges and Brains isn't just about resources, it's also about relationships."

Your companionship can be of huge value to someone. How can you perform community service in your town?

Friends are a sturdy shelter...a treasure...beyond price...life-saving. (Sirach 6:14,15,16)

Encourage us to be good neighbors and good friends, God.

Passion for Success

What's the secret of success?

You'll get different answers from different people, of course. Here's an interesting perspective from Walter Chrysler, the automaker who founded Chrysler Motors in the 1920's.

"The real secret of success is enthusiasm," he said. "Yes, more than enthusiasm, I would say is excitement. I like to see people get excited. When they get excited, they make a success of their lives.

"You can do anything if you have enthusiasm. Enthusiasm is the sparkle in your eye; it is the swing in your gait, the grip of your hand, the irresistible surge of your will and your energy to execute your ideas. Enthusiasts are fighters. They have fortitude, they have staying qualities. Enthusiasm is at the bottom of all progress. With it, there is accomplishment. Without it, there are only alibis."

Having enthusiasm, even passion, for life can make all the difference between merely surviving and actually thriving.

The God of heaven is the one who will give us success. (Nehemiah 2:20)

Fill me with a zest and zeal for doing Your will and living Your word all my days, Creator of all.

Going Green, One Pastry at a Time

The phrase "going green," or acting in an energy efficient or environmentally conscious way, has worked its way into our everyday lexicon.

Small businesses have worked the practice into their daily activities, too. Take the Little Cupcake Bake Shop in Bay Ridge, Brooklyn. The owners of the quaint cake and pastry shop have cut back their energy and water usage by installing energy-efficient windows, switching to biodegradable bags and utensils and adding a recycling unit in the dining area.

Initially, the owners had hesitated, but the customers surprised them with an overwhelmingly positive response: they like helping the environment and realize that cost savings by the owners translates into cost-containment for them.

Most people can be surprisingly flexible and open minded, if we just give them the chance.

Why do you see the speck in your neighbor's eye, but do not notice the log in your own eye? (Luke 6:41)

Discourage us from judging others, Father.

The Traveling Healers

A young mother in Juticalpa, Honduras, was preparing tortillas over a small fire pit while her young children played. One sibling gave a younger brother a playful push, and he stepped into a pot of boiling corn meal, resulting in severe burns.

Despite a dearth of local medical services the boy got the care he needed, thanks to Dr. Bill Runyon and his colleagues. Dr. Runyon, along with 30 other doctors and nurses, makes an annual, one-week medical missionary trip to small, rural towns like Juticalpa to try to meet the people's overwhelming medical needs.

"It's a drop in the bucket," admits Dr. Runyon, who provides remote villagers with seven days of non-stop medical care, often the only medical attention the patients receive in a year. But he also acknowledges, "We do save a lot of lives."

Remember that, depending on one's attitude, the most hopeless situations can hold the greatest potential for success.

Honor physicians for...their gift of healing comes from the Most High. (Sirach 38:1,2)

In difficult circumstances and trying times, increase our faith and optimism, God.

Bocce, Anyone?

Bocce ball is making a comeback especially among younger players and in suburban neighborhoods.

Basically, it's played with each of two teams using four balls weighing about three pounds each. The balls are rolled or tossed at a smaller, target ball called a pallino. A team scores points for each ball that gets closer to the pallino than its opponent.

While the early Romans were the first to play the game as it exists today, the sport has enjoyed strong appeal among older, Italian men in urban areas. Today, however, younger players have taken a liking to the game, especially those living near beaches, since the game can easily be played on sand.

Says one player, "In bocce, gender and age lines disappear." Even less-athletic players can find surprising agility at playing bocce.

Bocce represents a creative way to bridge gaps among different groups. What other creative way can you discover?

God created humankind in His image, in the image of God He created them; male and female He created them. (Genesis 1:27)

Clear my sight so I see what unites us, Lord, not what divides us.

God's Bailout

As the economy went into freefall, workers, those employed and others suddenly without jobs, turned to God for help.

Houses of worship in New York City began providing programs to help workers manage the stress of the stock market meltdown, including immediate counseling, job training and long-term direction for those who still had jobs but weren't sure for how long.

Rabbi Henry Harris with the Jewish outreach agency Aish has held emergency sessions for mainly entry-level employees worried about keeping their jobs and paying their bills. At Wall Street's Trinity Church, there are sessions on coping with stress in uncertain times.

In good times and in bad, God's loving counsel and strong arms are available to us. We need only open up to our compassionate Abba.

My steadfast love shall not depart from you, and My covenant of peace shall not be removed, says the Lord, who has compassion on you. (Isaiah 54:10)

Help me through times of distress, Abba.

Humorous Probabilities

S M I L E ! For heaven's sake, smile! It may seem like some strange law of nature, but have you noticed that:

- If you dial a wrong number someone always answers.
- If you change lines or traffic lanes, the one you left will always move faster.
- When you summon the techie or mechanic, the machine that would not work, will.
- The people whose seats are furthest from the aisle arrive last at any event.
- Any tool, when dropped, will roll to the least accessible corner.
- When you are fully immersed in your bath, either the phone or door bell will ring.
- Make an appointment to see your doctor because you don't feel well and you will be better by the time you get there.

Find the humor in each day. Laugh!

Our mouth was filled with laughter, and our tongue with shouts of joy. (Psalm 126:2)

Fill my life with laughter and joy, Jesus.

Choosing a Way of Life

What does it mean to follow your conscience; to choose right over wrong as a way of life?

The principal of a high school addressed a graduating class with these words: "We are told that we cannot judge actions as good or bad, white or black. Most are gray—and so we seek justification for whatever we do and deceive others into the thought that we are blameless. But do not be fooled. There is no half-measure. You cannot be half-honest, half decent or 'half-anything'.

"For every right, there is a corresponding duty; for every breach of the laws of God and humankind, there is a definite and certain punishment and retribution; for every action, there is personal responsibility."

Moral judgments are not always easy. But a wholehearted desire to follow God's will can help you know right from wrong and to choose the right course.

If you choose, you can keep the commandments, and to act faithfully is a matter of your own choice. (Sirach 15:15)

Paraclete, show me how to live to the best of my ability with integrity and courage, following Your path always.

Chef to the World — at Seven

They've prepared and shipped 30 million meals worldwide. But not one of these chefs is old enough to vote.

As part of Kids Against Hunger, young volunteers prepare specially formulated rice-soy casseroles for starving children and their families in more than 40 countries.

Don Fields started the program in Brighton, Iowa, in 2004, after making a mission trip with his wife to Honduras and seeing the hunger there.

The young chefs in Brighton alone have sent some 200,000 meals overseas, to places like Guatemala, Romania and Ethiopia. "It helps them so they won't die," says 7-year-old volunteer Noah.

Brianna, 15, says, "It's really fun to know you are making a difference in the world."

Our caring words and deeds can offer others hope and life.

As you did it to one of the least...members of My family, you did it to Me....As you did not do it to one of these, you did not do it to Me. (Matthew 25:40, 45)

Your love, Lord, renews and refreshes my soul. Show me how to share Your love.

Whole Living

Whole: from the Middle English *hool* healthy, unhurt, entire. So "whole living" is living that's healthy, entire, and not likely to hurt. Here, from *Body + Soul* Magazine, are some ideas for "whole living:"

- Let your soul weigh in on your decisions.
- Greet every day with a ritual of gratitude and strength.
- See love everywhere instead of seeking love.
- Believe in an abundant universe—your world will feel more plentiful.
- Make time to celebrate each day's small successes.
- See your limitations as opportunities to cultivate self-kindness.
- Remember that a resolution is a chance to move your life forward.
- Cultivate patience because the best kind of positive change comes gradually.

Your life is God's gift to you. Handle it with love.

To get wisdom is to love oneself.
(Proverbs 19:8)

Creator, help me acquire genuine wisdom.

God's Job Offer

After she finished college, Abigail Caperton of Texas had a difficult time deciding what she wanted to do with her life.

"Then, one Sunday after Mass, God approached me with a job offer," she recalls.

That day, God approached her through her soon-to-be-boss and fellow parishioner, Seth Morgan, who took her aside and spoke about starting an organization that would help support Catholic missionary groups and send others on short-term mission trips.

Orant (the name signifies a style of prayer portrayed in early Christian art) Charities began that Sunday after Mass, and has since sent many on trips to the developing world, while supporting the service of others among the world's poor and suffering.

Caperton herself has made missionary journeys. After a visit to Malawi, she said, "How blessed I feel to have witnessed such life-giving work."

God is calling each of us. Listen!

Give ear, O My people, to My teaching; incline your ears to the words of My mouth. (Psalm 78:1)

In all I say and do this day, may I reveal the Good News of Your great love, Lord.

Disney and Dali

In 1937, famed surrealist painter Salvador Dalí wrote to a friend, "I have come to Hollywood and am in touch with three great American surrealists—the Marx Brothers, Cecil B. DeMille, and Walt Disney."

It was the last of the three, the famed creator of Mickey Mouse, with whom Dalí teamed up on a short film called *Destino*. Unfortunately, financial troubles shelved the project, but, in 2003, Disney animators finished what Dalí started.

The film includes 150 storyboards, drawings and paintings which have sat for the last half-century in Disney vaults. The new *Destino* includes these works, incorporates some of Dalí's iconic images, including the melting clock, and adds motion.

The curator of the Gala-Salvador Dalí Foundation praised the result, calling it "the perfect combination of Dalí and Disney."

Working together on any project can make the most of the talents of all the people.

Two are better than one, because they have a good reward for their toil. For if they fall, one will lift up the other. (Ecclesiastes 4:9)

Be my support, Lord. Send me Your strength.

About Cows and History

James Knowlton starts each Fourth of July just as he does every day: milking the 55 Holsteins he and his father own.

Such actions belie the fact that his ancestry includes forebears who played a part in the early history of this nation. Lieutenant Colonel Thomas Knowlton, for one, was an American patriot who served during the Revolutionary and the French and Indian Wars.

The Connecticut dairy farmer first learned of the exploits of Colonel Knowlton from his fourth-grade teacher. Before that, he thought the tales his grandfather told him were "just family stories."

When Knowlton has children of his own, he says that he will teach them about their courageous ancestors and the liberties for which they so boldly fought.

Our own past is filled with triumphs, as well as trials. All help shape us for the future and in our everyday.

Tell of it, you who ride on white donkeys, you who sit on rich carpets and you who walk by the way. To the sound of musicians...repeat the triumphs of the Lord. (Judges 5:10-11)

Remind us that Your loving presence is with us always, Lord, yesterday, today and forever.

An Unlikely, Yet Well-Matched Pair

If Abraham Lincoln and Mary Todd were alive and courting today, the tabloids would have a field day. Lincoln was a towering, self-educated, rough-hewn Illinoisan. Todd was short in stature, wealthy, dainty, and secure in her role as a Southern belle.

Todd's sister, among others, found the couple peculiar, and few close to them believed it a good match. Rumor had it that Todd's temper made her husband's life miserable.

But historians, such as Doris Kearns Goodwin, find it remarkable that such an unfounded myth persists. "I don't know how many women Lincoln could have found who would have loved both politics and poetry as she did," she says.

Perhaps Lincoln's own words are all that matter. He said his marriage to Todd was "a matter of profound wonder."

Marriage is a matter of "profound wonder." Two strangers build a life together "for better, for worse, for richer, for poorer, in sickness and in health, until death do them part."

Love is strong as death, passion fierce as the grave. ...Many waters cannot quench love, neither can floods drown it.
(Song of Solomon 8:6,7)

Counselor, guide couples on their journey.

Little Things and Caring

The little things in life matter. Here are two examples:

After Peggy Frezon's mother was diagnosed with breast cancer, Frezon realized she herself was at greater risk. Because she often postponed her annual mammogram, Frezon decided to schedule her annual mammogram on her mother's birthday.

"What could be a better birthday gift for any mother than knowing that her daughter is taking care of her health?"

When Ora McGuire moved to Walpole, Massachusetts, she found a consignment clothing store, Second Glance. The owner, Diane, greeted her with a smile and helped her choose ideal clothes. Later McGuire learned that twice a year, when Diane restocks her shop, she gives away the last of her inventory to needy people and local churches.

It *is* the little things we do for ourselves and others that count in life.

Are not five sparrows sold for two pennies? Yet not one of them is forgotten in God's sight. (Luke 12:6)

Remind me, Abba, of the importance of small, seemingly insignificant things.

Camp Read-a-Lot

Eastern Kentucky is home to 14 of the poorest counties in the United States. The Lexington, Kentucky Episcopal Diocese, was aware of this disturbing statistic and the connection between poverty and education. The Diocese understood how children benefit from early intervention in education, especially reading.

To help these children, the Diocese launched a summer reading camp that offers free, personalized, intensive reading instruction for three hours, followed by fun activities.

The model for this ministry has since caught on in other areas. Today, a dozen other U.S. dioceses and churches, as well as some churches as far away as South Africa, are employing the same model.

Poverty affects people in a multitude of ways beginning in infancy and childhood. How can poverty begin to be alleviated in your community? Literacy programs are a start.

Show kindness and mercy...do not oppress the widow, the orphan, the alien, or the poor; and do not devise evil...against one another. (Zechariah 7:9,10)

Infuse your people with generosity, Father God.

An Unlikely Olympian

Laura Wilkinson would be the first to admit she's not your typical Olympic athlete. She's 5'6", not her competitors' 4'10." She's twice as old as many platform divers and didn't begin diving until age 15. "I feel I should walk out onto the platform with a cane," she jokes.

Despite her self-deprecating humor, Wilkinson sees platform diving as a form of worship. "Worship is using our gifts to glorify God," she says. "So diving to the best of my abilities feels like worship to me."

Wilkinson's approach to failure is also unusual. She won gold medals at Sydney's 2000 Olympics, but is "learning to be thankful even when I'm disappointed or upset. I trust God has a plan, and the peace that comes from completely trusting Him is like nothing else on earth."

While there are many ways to express one's love for God, trust is always one of them.

Trust in the Lord with all your heart. (Proverbs 3:5)

Calm my soul with childlike faith in You, Mighty Lord.

Fighting for the Helpless with Faith

Think of Indonesia, and the image of lush jungles and abundant fauna likely come to mind. Sadly, in recent years, aggressive logging practices are decimating trees, and poachers are killing or trafficking in wild animals, many of which are members of endangered species.

Indonesian biologist and Muslim, Rosek Nursahid, founder of ProFauna, a nature conservancy organization, works to counter this. Christians, Hindus, Muslims, and other ProFauna volunteers find themselves immersed in a holistic experience in environmental custodianship. Activism includes rescuing animals, encouraging enforcement of Indonesian environmental laws, and confronting animal traffickers. And there's education in environmental awareness and respect for animals—classes and camps for students, teachers, government officials and others.

People of different faiths *can* find a common ground. Focus on what unites, rather than what can potentially divide.

I am establishing my covenant with you and your descendants...and with every living creature. (Genesis 9:9,10)

Bring all your children together, God of the Covenant.

The Importance of Saying "I'm Sorry"

More than anything, Samuel Snow wanted an apology. Snow and 27 other black World War II soldiers had been convicted of the death of an Italian prisoner of war.

In 2007, after Congress ordered a review, the Army overturned the men's convictions and sent them checks for the pay they would have received, although without interest.

So it wasn't the fact that the Army sent Samuel Snow a check for only $725 based on his pay at the time of his conviction that bothered him. He believed he deserved an apology. Finally, at a ceremony sixty-four years after they had been wrongfully convicted, an assistant secretary for the Army apologized to the men and their families for the "grievous wrong."

Although too sick to attend the ceremony, Snow heard about the apology and "had a smile so big," said his son.

Three little words, "I am sorry," can make a difference in another's life.

With the judgment you make you will be judged, and the measure you give will be the measure you get. (Matthew 7:2)

Strengthen individuals, corporations and governments to take responsibility for their words and actions, Lord.

Protecting the Helpless

Brain-damaged and partially paralyzed, Joshua DeShaney doesn't know he's now 30 years old. DeShaney relies completely on others in a home for profoundly retarded and disabled adults in Wisconsin.

Born a healthy, bright child in 1979, DeShaney's young parents soon divorced, and Joshua was put in his father's custody. His ex-wife and police believed DeShaney's father abused him. County social workers documented the child's frequent extensive injuries. Yet no one removed DeShaney from his father.

Then two weeks before his fifth birthday, DeShaney's father beat him into a coma. He survived with massive brain damage that left him partially paralyzed and profoundly retarded.

If you suspect a child (or an adult) is being abused physically, spiritually, emotionally or mentally, speak out. Remember, respect-filled love and abuse never co-exist.

Jesus said..."It would be better for you if a millstone were hung around your neck and you were thrown into the sea than for you to cause one of these little ones to stumble."
(Luke 17:1,2)

Merciful God, give us the courage to speak for abused children and adults.

More Than Meets the Eye

In 1989, optometrist Doug Villella had what he calls "the transformative experience" of his life. At the suggestion of a priest, Villella went on a 10-day retreat to learn how to center his prayer life. The result: "My desire to serve in the Third World was a spontaneous interest that arose from the depths of my prayer experience," says Villella.

Soon after, he joined Volunteer Optometric Services to Humanity of Pennsylvania, a branch of the international organization that has 34 regional chapters worldwide, and he went on his first mission trip.

Since then, Villella and his co-volunteers have served thousands of needy people in Guatemala and Haiti, providing basic eye care, medical treatment, and medication to the poor.

Villella took action to bring his prayers to life. How can you deepen and enliven your prayers—and bring them to life?

**I sought wisdom openly in my prayer.
(Sirach 51:13)**

Jesus, teach us how to walk in faith, in action.

Steak at the Soup Kitchen

It's one-of-a-kind, say its operators. The Masbia Soup Kitchen in Borough Park, Brooklyn, serves only hot kosher meals—some 160 of them in fact, five nights a week.

And on one day a year, steak is on the menu. The unusual offering is in honor of Grand Rabbi Yeshaya Steiner of Kerestir, Hungary, who died in 1925 and was known for feeding the hungry and other acts of charity.

Even the decor makes this soup kitchen different. The setup resembles a restaurant. There are tall plants and dividers for dining privacy.

Co-founder Alexander Rapaport explains, "We try to treat everyone equal: There's a saying that even in the synagogue, the fishmonger sits with the stockbroker."

In our lifetime, we're called to give, and we may also know what it means to be in need. Learn lessons from all circumstances.

Loose the bonds of injustice. ...Let the oppressed go free. ...Share your bread with the hungry. (Isaiah 58:6,7)

Remind the wealthy and the indigent that before You, Just Judge, they are equal in dignity and worth.

Good Sportsmanship For Parents

You probably encourage your children to participate in sports, perhaps your favorite sport, because you found it rewarding and think they will, too. They'll boost their self confidence; learn cooperation and teamwork; get a feeling of camaraderie; be part of a trusted support system; and learn better communication.

Just remember that nothing can change your children's basic natures.

Here are tips for parents of young athletes:

- Offer constructive criticism gently.
- Give sincere praise, win, lose or tie, with a smile.
- Be happy if your children are having fun.
- Lack of success is not fatal. Don't micromanage your children.
- If your child wants to quit a sport, keep an open mind.

Let sports be fun.

Train children in the right way. (Proverbs 22:6)

Jesus, who played games with the other children of Nazareth, help children find enjoyment in all they do.

The Love That Shaped a Cardinal

On his deathbed, Cardinal Henry Edward Manning penned these words: "Into this little book my dearest wife wrote her prayers and meditations.—All the good I may have done, all the good I may have been, I owe to her." Manning, as an Anglican priest, had been wed to Caroline Sargent. Their marriage was blissfully happy, but tragically short.

After her death, and numerous visits to Rome and conversations with Catholic friends, Manning entered the Catholic Church in 1851. He was re-ordained and eventually became head of the Catholic Church in England.

"Not a day has passed since her death on which I have not prayed and meditated from this book," the dying cardinal said, revealing his late wife's profound influence on one of the English Catholic Church's greatest leaders.

A committed relationship enriches the spouses' lives immeasurably even after death has separated them.

Let the heavens and the whole creation bless You forever. You made Adam, and for him you made his wife Eve. (Tobit 8:5-6)

Holy God, bless engaged and married couples. May they love one another for time and for eternity.

Urban Honey

Wine aficionados are known to enjoy a "flight" of wines, or a small tasting of several different wines. Now, it seems, those with a sweet tooth are adopting the tradition with a tasting flight of global honeys.

Andrew Cóte, an inveterate traveler and beekeeper, has collected a remarkable array of rare and exquisite honeys from Lithuania, Israel, and even Manhattan's Lower East Side and elsewhere around the world.

"I'm trying to figure out which weeds grow in lots and alleys near rooftop beehives to give the honey its distinctive taste," he explains. Cóte has also managed to turn his unusual hobby into charitable works. He founded "Bees Without Borders," a non-profit aid program that teaches beekeeping in impoverished areas worldwide.

How can you leverage your gifts for the benefit of others?

O that My people would listen to Me...I would feed you with the finest of the wheat, and with honey. (Psalm 81:13,16)

Guide me toward selflessness and generosity, Lamb of God.

Living a Little Lower on the Hog

When Kyle Kramer and his family spend a muggy summer without air conditioning, growing and preserving their own food, it isn't because they hate technology.

"I love my iPod," Kramer writes, but he believes we need to change our habits. "We will not navigate our way toward a socially and ecologically sustainable future without personal and communal sacrifice," he writes in *America*.

"Whether we choose to make sacrifices out of solidarity and moral conviction or are forced to do so by some ecological or economic collapse, we in the first world countries will soon have to start living much less high on the hog."

Asceticism's "deeper fruit is a softer heart: gratitude and a sense of solidarity that leads to compassion."

Let's take steps to live more simply and justly even if that means some deprivation, discomfort, and self-denial.

(Jesus) said to them, "Take care! Be on your guard against all kinds of greed; for one's life does not consist in the abundance of possessions." (Luke 12:15)

Open my clenched fists, Jesus. Help me learn the difference between need and greed.

Cooking for Refugees

Janice Kamenir-Reznick wanted to do something about the genocide in Darfur in the Sudan. So she founded a company called Solar Cookers International—and provided solar-powered pots to refugees from the Sudanese genocide.

The retired environmental lawyer knew that women and children faced horrific dangers—gang rape, enslavement, murder—when they ventured out in the bush to gather firewood for cooking. The CooKit is easy-to-assemble and inexpensive, just $15 each. And it reduces trips to collect firewood, decreases the number of assaults and helps food taste better because it is smokeless.

"Until we started this organization," says Kamenir-Reznick, "I believed that Darfur was a faraway problem, one that I couldn't fix. But now nobody can say that there's nothing they can do about it."

Because we are all children in God's family, we are called to embrace our neighbors' problems as though they were our own.

Store up almsgiving in your treasury, and it will rescue you from every disaster. (Sirach 29:12)

We are all Your children, Father. Help me to always see the world as neighborhood.

A Summer of Service

Their motivation was simple: help feed the hungry. The young men and women of the St. Joseph Church youth group in Scituate, Rhode Island, could have spent their summer hanging out, traveling or pursuing other leisure activities.

Instead, they used pitchforks, carried huge wicker baskets of produce and otherwise worked to ensure that a local food pantry was amply stocked to feed the hungry.

One group member, Colleen McCormick, emphasizes that people don't have to leave their own communities to find others who need help. Carissa Ricciarelli, another member, added, "It really makes me feel good when I help someone." Matthew Fantasia said he was glad to be part of an effort to put food on hungry people's tables. "It's what all parishes should do," he says.

Give young people the opportunity to make an impact. They may surprise you.

The measure you give will be the measure you get back. (Luke 6:38)

Remind me, Jesus, that snap judgments are unfair and hurtful.

"Last Lecture" Inspires Many

If you knew you had only a short time to live, what would you do? A sobering thought, but one that computer-science professor Randy Pausch had to face when his pancreatic cancer worsened.

Rather than wallow in self-pity, Pausch gave a lecture on the wisdom he'd impart if he knew it was his last chance, as indeed, it was. He spoke of childlike wonder and his love for his wife and children. Soon, his lecture spread across the Web and was translated into many languages.

Pausch lost his battle with cancer in July 2008. Millions have been touched by his lecture. Many say he'd inspired them to quit feeling sorry for themselves, or to pay more attention to their families. One woman said Pausch's words gave her the strength to escape an abusive relationship; another, not to commit suicide.

Every moment of your life is God's gift. Appreciate it!

Blessed are the dead who...die in the Lord. ...They will rest from their labors, for their deeds follow them. (Revelation 14:13)

Thank you for Your gift of life, Divine Wisdom.

It Started on a Japanese Street

In 1959, while performing in Japan on a goodwill tour for American troops there, Sara O'Meara and Yvonne Fedderson met a group of cold and frightened children, the offspring of American soldiers and Japanese women, who were living on the streets.

Immediately, their hearts were moved to an act of kindness that would eventually benefit thousands. The performers found a local woman to care for these unwanted, abandoned children. They offered financial help as well.

As more of these American-Japanese kids were found, the two started fundraising, sending support and providing for similar outreach back home in the United States. Today, their Childhelp organization, which developed from that 1959 meeting on a Japanese street, is dedicated to helping victims of child abuse and neglect as well as at-risk children.

Every encounter holds within it the opportunity to right a wrong; to do good.

Jesus...said, "Let the little children come to Me, and do not stop them; for it is to such as these that the kingdom of God belongs. (Luke 18:16)

Jesus, help me see You in poor, neglected and unwanted infants and children. Guide my actions on their behalf.

Bridging the Gap — Within

Della Mae Justice defied the odds. She was born in an Appalachian "holler," a small valley within the lush mountains and creeks of Kentucky. Her family lived for years without indoor plumbing or a regular income. Her father was absent, and her older half-brother often hunted squirrels so the family could eat.

Hungry for a better life, Justice worked her way out of Appalachia. She made her way through college and law school and has traveled Europe as she's moved up the ladder in her legal career.

Yet, when she returns home, she feels out of place: her life has changed profoundly, altering the way people view her. At the same time, as she advanced in her profession, Justice felt like an outsider among those from more privileged beginnings. Today, she continues to bridge the gap, aware of both the boon and bane of her success.

Be open to the people around you as unique individuals.

Do not judge by appearances, but judge with right judgment. (John 7:24)

Teach us to discard prejudices and to judge people by their intellect and actions, Holy Spirit.

Farm Fresh Feast

A handful of chefs are busy—on a truck with a stove, a smoker, refrigeration and a sink. It's time for Dinners at the Farm.

The brainchild of Connecticut chefs Drew McLachlan and Jonathan Rapp, the events serve up gourmet meals from local foods. The tab paid by diners benefits local non-profits. Some 160 people turned out for the first dinners, netting $17,000 for charity. Now, dinners happen three days in a row each month for four months.

"It's a win-win to have local produce, local meats and so forth, as well as you're helping something local out," says Brian Carey, a contractor, who attended two dinners. Adds Pauline Lord, whose farm served as a host, "It's such a great combination of elements."

Each of us is created to contribute just the right ingredient to make the world around us a better place.

To each is given the manifestation of the Spirit for the common good. To one...wisdom, and to another...knowledge...to another faith...to another gifts of healing. (1 Corinthians 12:7,8,9)

You give us from Your bounty, Eternal Father. May we reverence the works of Your hands.

Going Global — at Home

Would you rather see the world or save the world? As concerns over global warming heat up, some travelers are debating the environmental impact of air travel. Many are opting to vacation locally to make a positive impact globally.

Global Cool, an organization dedicated to fighting global warming, says that visitors to its web site have pledged to cut enough air travel to reduce carbon emissions by a combined 2,205 tons, the equivalent of about 1,770 round-trip flights between New York and Los Angeles!

Sev and Nina Williams of California have sworn off air travel for a while. Rather than the five airplane trips they took last year, the couple plans to spend this year's vacation visiting local eateries and enjoying their neighborhood. "We looked at our whole life and asked, 'How can we make an impact?'" says Sev Williams.

Protect our planet in every way you can. It's the only home we've got!

The earth is the Lord's and all that is in it...for He has founded it...and established it. (Psalm 24:1,2)

Creator, may we express our gratitude for our exquisite planet tailored to our needs by caring for it as a mother for her child.

Tuning Into Life

As David Hochman approached 40, he felt a craving to play a musical instrument, again. "My path to musical greatness was diverted roughly 30 years ago," Hochman says, noting that he gave up piano lessons, and his crabby piano teacher, at age 11.

A gift of a mandolin on his 40th birthday led to hours of picking and playing in his living room, but all alone. Then a search of the Internet uncovered Dr. Banjo, Pete Wernick and his musical "jam" camp in Boulder, Colorado. "The only way to learn to play and keep playing is by playing with other people," Wernick says.

The time in Colorado also taught Hochman a life lesson. "Jamming, like life itself, is about playing through your mistakes," he says.

Facing our mistakes or our problems is always easier with the loving support of others.

Associate with a godly person whom you know to be a keeper of the commandments, who is like-minded with yourself. (Sirach 37:12)

I sing Your praises, Lord, for all You have given me.

On One Small Bench

Nobel laureate writer Toni Morrison has said that her acclaimed novel, *Beloved*, was born of her desire to recognize slaves' history and suffering. In an interview, Morrison said, "There is no suitable memorial, plaque, wreath, wall or small bench by the road" that commemorates the long and painful story of slavery in America.

Finally, in 2008, the long-awaited "bench by the road" became a reality. Under a blazing South Carolina sun, Morrison, and some 300 supporters, gathered as she dedicated a six-foot long steel bench. "It's never too late to honor the dead," said Morrison.

This bench on Sullivan's Island faces South Carolina's Intracoastal Waterway, which was a primary entry point for nearly 40 per cent of the millions of enslaved Africans in the U.S. "We have come back to the place we started from," said one supporter.

Honor and remember those who have suffered and endured. Work for interracial justice and respect.

Act with justice and righteousness...do no wrong or violence to the alien, the orphan, and the widow. (Jeremiah 22:3)

God, forgive us for building much of our nation on the sweat and tears of slaves.

An Armful of Hope

It's become almost commonplace for people to have organ donations. Yet it made headlines when a 54-year-old German farmer had the world's first double arm transplant in July, 2008.

Karl Merk lost both his arms just below the shoulders in a terrible combine harvester accident about six years before then. It took 40 surgeons, anesthesiologists, nurses and other support staff to perform the 15-hour operation at the Munich University Clinic. Within months Merk was able to handle simple tasks such as opening doors and switching lights on and off. Eventually, he hopes to be able to care for himself again and even ride a motorcycle.

"It was really overwhelming when I saw that I had arms again," says Merk. "These are my arms, and I'm not giving them away again."

Medical and scientific breakthroughs offer many opportunities that never existed before. Let's be grateful and use them well to benefit all God's children.

Honor physicians for...the Lord created them. ...The Lord created medicines...and the sensible will not despise them. (Sirach 38:1,4)

Thank You, Compassionate Father, for helping us use Your gifts for the good of Your people.

The Gift of Good Food

From the time chef Alice Waters opened a restaurant over 30 years ago in Berkeley, California, chefs and home cooks began to embrace her philosophy: eat local, eat seasonal, eat organic.

"It's strange when people talk about global warming, and don't think about how we eat as a factor," says Waters. Many don't realize that processing and transporting food contributes to pollution. Fortunately, interest in organic food has expanded. Also, organic farm acreage has quadrupled.

Waters has also created an Edible Schoolyard at the Martin Luther King Jr. Middle School in Berkeley. While the children tend and harvest the garden, they "grow their lunch and learn that good food comes from the earth, not a vending machine."

Eating organically will not only promote better health for you and your family, it will also decrease pollution and global warming. Try to eat locally and seasonally.

God said, "See, I have given you every plant yielding seed that is upon the...earth, and every tree with seed in its fruit; you shall have them for food. (Genesis 1:29)

Bless our smallest efforts, Lord of all.

A Final Salute for a Champion

A mile-and-a-half-long procession through Harlem followed a memorial service at New York City's Riverside Church one day in July, 2008. A horse-drawn carriage carried the coffin. And there was even an elephant.

"She was very fond of elephants, especially with their trunks up," said someone who participated in these events honoring Barbara Ann Teer, founder of the National Black Theatre, who died at 71.

Founded in 1968, the NBT produced entertainment, art exhibitions and special events, and toured the world from its home base in New York City's Harlem. "Barbara championed our culture," said Basil A. Paterson, former state senator and deputy mayor, before a crowd that filled the church. Teer is credited with keeping black theater alive in the city.

Our life's actions should always reflect our pride in our self, our culture, our family, our beliefs and our standards.

O families of the peoples, ascribe to the Lord glory and strength...the glory due His name; bring an offering, and come into His courts. (Psalm 96:7,8)

Help me, Blessed Trinity, to live my life as You want me to live it, with quiet self-esteem.

Get Green

Want to help your planet, yourself, and others? Go green!

"There's been a major shift in attitude," says Robbie Cox, president of the Sierra Club, the nation's oldest environmental group, "People realize they *can* make a difference." By making little changes in your daily activities and at home, you can make a positive difference in the world.

Here are some suggestions from *Glamour* magazine:

Recycle and Reuse: less energy will be wasted fabricating new items and less pollution will be released.

Shop online: every minute spent driving to a store uses ten times the energy used to shop by computer.

Help eliminate plastic: buy a reusable water bottle or install a home filter.

Use green power: find an energy company that uses wind, sun, or water for power.

Try these ideas yourself. Share them with others.

It is required of stewards that they be found trustworthy. (1 Corinthians 4:2)

Remind us, Creator, to be good stewards of Your earth, our home.

What's for Lunch?

That's a question you've probably asked or answered many times. But for the 48 percent of Boone County, Indiana, students on a government-subsidized lunch program this question is especially vital during school breaks.

With the help of churches and local organizations, money is collected, and food is bought and packaged for the What's For Lunch? program which provides five lunches each week from the start of the summer until the new school year begins.

Ingrid Temple, chairwoman of the Shalom Community, said she had heard about children going hungry once school was over and even having to ask for food. It was time for a change. What's for Lunch? fulfills the meaning of Shalom's name, peace, by encouraging people from different faith traditions to cooperate for a worthy cause.

Helping needy children can be as easy as packing lunches!

Come, you that are blessed by My Father...for I was hungry and you gave Me food, I was thirsty and you gave Me something to drink. (Matthew 25:34,35)

Jesus living and life-giving bread, how can I help remedy the scourge of hunger in this nation and around the world?

Avoiding Burnout

Chronically exhausted? Angry? Cynical, negative and irritable? Frequent headaches or gastrointestinal upsets? Sleepless? Depressed? Suspicious?

Rest in God to avoid burnout. Begin each day with praise of the Creator. Excerpts from the Psalms are great.

Keep a day of complete rest, a Sabbath, one day each week. No television, computers, radios, cell phones.

Seek out laughter. Enjoy humor.

Meditate. Embrace silence, stillness simplicity.

Repeat affirmations throughout the day.

Don't take yourself, others, or life so seriously.

Consider the advice of Martin Luther who said, "if I did not spend two or three hours each day in prayer, I would not get through the day."

Life is God's precious gift to you. Don't waste it in endless work, bitterness and fretfulness.

Come to Me, all you that are weary and are carrying heavy burdens, and I will give you rest. (Matthew 11:28)

Jesus, help me to sit gladly at Your feet delighting in Your company.

Recording Their Way to Recovery

Looking at Madison Keel, standing at ease in front of a microphone in a recording studio, one would think she was a child performer. Keel, however, is fighting acute leukemia at Texas Children's Hospital, in a rather unconventional way: by recording her own songs.

Thanks to the inspiration of Houston pianist and composer Anita Kruse, the Children's Cancer Center of Baylor College of Medicine and Texas Children's Hospital has a music studio where 85 children so far have recorded their songs as part of their unique path to recovery and healing.

"The arts have therapeutic value," says Dr. David G. Poplack, the center's director. Getting young cancer patients to express themselves musically can be particularly helpful to their recovery.

Healing comes in many ways. Sharing your talents with others can be one way. The benefits can be amazing.

Whenever the evil spirit...came upon Saul, David took the lyre and played it...and Saul would be relieved and feel better, and the evil spirit would depart from him. (1 Samuel 16:23)

Instill me with the discipline to nurture my talents, Paraclete.

Pesky, Peculiar, Persistent

Birders "ooh" and "ahh" at wrens and herons, but often find woodpeckers annoying despite their beauty.

While that reputation is somewhat justified since the woodpecker's efforts at nest-building often result in noise and home damage, a closer look may shed a more favorable light on them. Says a utilities worker, "I see a lot of woodpecker damage where power, cable and phone lines attach. I think they mistake the hum of the wires for insects."

Twan Leenders, a conservation biologist for Connecticut's Audubon Society, adds "they're in need of a certain amount of fat, especially around nesting time," hence their quest to find insects. He also believes that the woodpecker's penchant for pecking on metal gutters is done "to attract females and scare away other males."

Prejudice results from misconceptions. Before you make snap judgments, take a closer look. The facts will surprise you.

By streams the birds...have their habitation; they sing among the branches. (Psalm 104:12)

Dear God, how beautiful each species of bird! What a joy to hear them; to see their flocks flung against the sky; to mark the weather and seasons by them!

Time Out...for Parents

Karen saw the two couples every Sunday afternoon. They would come to her husband's café, each with a young daughter in tow. It was nearly impossible for the adults to enjoy the soothing music of the weekly jazz performance.

On this one Sunday, Karen had an idea. She offered her own pre-teen daughter double her allowance that week, if she would take the younger girls from the couple into the café's office area and play some of the many games Karen kept there for her own grandchildren.

"Don't worry about the money mom," said Karen's daughter. "I'll do it for free."

Everyone had a good afternoon that Sunday...all enjoying moments of laughter, fun and friendship.

Life's joyous moments...however brief... energize the spirit and refresh the soul.

A joyful heart is life itself. (Sirach 30:22)

I am filled with joy, Creator, and blessed by all You have given me.

Excuse Me, Pardon Me...

New York City has been called the Big Apple and the City That Never Sleeps. Lately though, the great city on the Hudson may well earn the nickname "The City of Hectic Streets."

A debate currently rages over the ever-growing congestion—cars, trucks, cyclists, joggers, strollers or even roller-skaters. Something has got to give. Here are some of the possible solutions with which city planners have been wrestling:

- Designate "Woonerfs." This Dutch word roughly translates as "living streets," where pedestrians would be on a par with cars, and speed bumps would slow cars to a crawl for greater safety.

- Create "Bicycle Boulevards." While less than one per cent of New Yorkers bike to work, this plan would encourage cycling.

- Designate "Play Streets." This would close entire streets so kids could play.

Everyone needs to slow down, calm down and rest, including the city that "never sleeps!"

Stand at the crossroads...ask for the ancient paths, where the good way lies; and walk in it, and find rest for your souls. (Jeremiah 6:16)

May Your presence give my soul rest, Jesus.

Disarming Prayer

What can one person do in the face of nuclear weapons? According to Fatima Portugal and Miriam Benedict of St. Charles Borromeo Catholic Church in Albuquerque, New Mexico, you might consider a novena, or nine days of special prayer.

The women put together a Novena for Peace and Disarmament which brought together various parish groups and included Mass celebrated in four languages: English, Spanish, Vietnamese and American Sign Language. Local peace groups made presentations.

"I'm still overwhelmed by the number of people who came out to pray for peace," said Blessed Sacrament pastor Father John Thomas Lane. "We recognized how we are all connected to each other."

Our prayers for disarmament have a ripple effect. Each prayer adds to those of many.

The effect of righteousness will be peace, and the result of righteousness, quietness and trust forever. (Isaiah 32:17)

Holy Spirit, show us how to live in righteousness and peace.

Faith's Gift

More than six years ago a litter of puppies was born. Several were dead. One was trapped beneath its mother, its one front leg so deformed it couldn't walk. Reuben Stringfellow brought it home and named her Faith.

He and his family encouraged her to hone her balance and dexterity, and then get moving.

Today, Faith hops to a three-quarters upright stance using her head in a wave-like-motion as well as all of her abdominal muscles. She also visits amputees at Walter Reed Medical Center. One said he'd focus on what Faith had done and what he could do. Another kept a photo of her in his hospital room until he walked out on his artificial legs. In appreciation Faith was commissioned an E5 sergeant and given a U. S. Army uniform.

Animals can encourage us to live life come what may, because life is God's enjoyable gift.

Ask the animals, and they will teach you; the birds...will tell you....Plants...will teach....Fish... will declare...(that) in His hand is the life of every living thing. (Job 12:7,8,10)

Sustainer, give me the wise humility to learn from Your creatures the sheer joy of living.

A Real Risk

Do you take chances? A *Consumer Reports* survey of 1000 people found that people take lots of risks.

For example, even though we've heard about the dangers of prolonged exposure to the sun and the fact that a million new cases of skin cancer were reported in 2008, 27 per cent of respondents never use sunscreen. Using a bicycle helmet reduces the chance of head injury by 85 percent, but more than half of those in the survey never wear them. Rubber bath mats? Sixty-one percent must never worry about falling because they never use them.

Maybe they feel that they are the exception to the rule. Unfortunately, the odds are against them.

Instead of taking a risk with your health and safety, take a real chance on yourself—open your spirit to the wonders and possibilities with which God has blessed you in this awe-inspiring world of ours.

Consider the lilies, how they grow...I tell you, even Solomon in all his glory was not clothed like one of these. (Luke 12:27)

Show me how to revel in Your goodness, generous God, without taking pointless chances.

Miss Tradition and Culture?

Beauty pageants, which have been around for decades, have been known to evoke both interest and criticism. But in Jayuya, Puerto Rico, girls aged six through 16 can compete to win the honor of the girl who best symbolizes Puerto Rico's native Indian tribe, the Taino, based on her handmade outfits and her ties to Puerto Rico's indigenous culture.

Puerto Ricans have long considered themselves a mix of African, European and Native American peoples. Since the 1960s, Puerto Ricans have directed their pride toward the Taino, a tribe eliminated from the Antilles by conquest, disease and assimilation. Today, each year, the town of Jayuya celebrates its cultural beginnings through a competition that emphasizes understanding and appreciation for its roots.

What are your roots? How can you celebrate your understanding and appreciation for them?

Let us now sing the praises of...our ancestors in their generations. (Sirach 44:1)

Father, give my ancestors the rest in Your blessed presence for which they labored and longed.

Apart from the Crowd

Derrick Braxton seems to stand out from the crowd. Growing up in a public housing project in Crown Heights, Brooklyn, he chose not to hang out with local boys who joined gangs and used drugs. He thrived in high school.

Then Braxton followed the advice of a high school advisor and applied for a grant to attend college. Awarded the money, he found out he was the only applicant for the grant and one of the few young men from his neighborhood to attend college.

When Braxton chose Finger Lakes Community College in upstate New York, he again stood out because he was one of the few students who came from a public housing project.

A person's beginnings do not always determine their story's end. Sometimes, those with the most challenging circumstances have a superior drive and appreciation for turning their lives around.

Amos answered Amaziah, "I am no prophet, nor a prophet's son; but I am a herdsman, and a dresser of sycamore trees, and the Lord took me from following the flock, and...said to me, 'Go, prophesy'. (Amos 7:14-15)

Remind me never to judge others, Father, as I have neither walked in their shoes nor felt their pain and joy.

A New Place to Call Home

When native Hawaiians Sister Jane Francis Leandro and Sister Rose Henry Reeves first moved to Calcutta in 1991 to work as missionaries, the transition was difficult. Sister Jane Francis was distressed by the crowds, the squalor and destitution.

Yet, they were on a mission. They were the first Sacred Hearts Sisters to work there, assisting those with Hansen's disease, or leprosy. Before long, they were organizing intensive charitable efforts and directing volunteers in a number of initiatives.

In time, the Sisters found that their new home had enlightening surprises for them.

Says Sister Jane Francis, "Every person you meet in India has a reverence for God," along with a deep respect for any person or thing they consider holy. "If they know you are there in the service of God, they respect and protect you."

Have you kept your respect for the divine in its every manifestation?

In the beginning...a wind from God swept over the face of the waters. (Genesis 1:1)

Remind me to respect every person and religion and all creatures and Creation, Spirit which brooded over creation at the beginning.

Questions on Going Green

You already know the phrase, "reduce, reuse, recycle." So, before you buy anything, ask yourself if you absolutely love it; if you already have something similar; if the item saves you time or space.

Ask, too, where you will store it, if the price and quality are the best and whether or not you need to do more research before buying it.

This same routine is useful when cleaning closets. Ask if each item has a purpose, if you've used it within the last year, and whether it's a duplicate of something else. If it's broken ask yourself when you will have it repaired. And, finally, ask if looking at or using the item makes you happy.

There's nothing wrong with having things *if* you come to know how little you really need and what satisfies most. A greener life is a simpler, richer, deeper life.

Do not keep striving for what you are to eat and what you are to drink, and do not keep worrying....Your Father knows that you need them. (Luke 12:30)

Abba, help me grow in appreciation for the greener, simpler, richer life.

Gedenk...Remembers

If you think that a musician known as "The Hip-Hop Violinist" would have some unusual accomplishments, you'd be right.

Miri Ben-Ari was born in Tel Aviv, Israel, and studied under master violinist Isaac Stern. At age 19, she moved to New York and was drawn to the jazz scene where she started performing with popular artists like Wyclef Jean and Alicia Keys.

At the same time, Ben-Ari, a granddaughter of Nazi concentration camp survivors, was growing concerned that today's young people know little about the Holocaust. So she started Gedenk, an organization to educate teens. The Yiddish word means "remember."

"God gave us the ability to remember so that we wouldn't repeat past mistakes," says Miri Ben-Ari, "so that we would grow stronger from our experiences, no matter how horrific they may have been, so that we can build a brighter future."

For tomorrow's sake, remember the past.

I remember the days of old...all Your deeds... the works of Your hands. I stretch out my hands to You; my soul thirsts for You. (Psalm 143:5-6)

Teach me to value those who have come before me and those who will come after me by leading a good life, gracious Father.

...to Help Broken Children

North Carolinian Stacy Hannon thought she'd never forget the image: a 14-pound, 8-month-old baby boy in a body cast because of his biological father's abuse. Then she learned that a local children's shelter was being closed. With little money, no job, a recently laid-off husband and two children, Hannon still set out to raise money and awareness.

She started Strong Arms for Children, an arm-wrestling showcase that attracted 35 participants and even more observers. Attendees gave over $500 which she says "came from their hearts, not their wallets." And while Hannon lost her own wrestling match, the children at local shelters won community awareness to save the shelters; a truckload of toys and, yes, money. Hannon's prize? She met Jay, the battered boy who had inspired her and who was then a healthy toddler awaiting adoption.

It doesn't take much to make a difference. Modest efforts can have a huge impact.

It was I who taught Ephraim to walk, I took them up in My arms. ...I led them with cords of human kindness, with bands of love. ...I bent down to them and fed them. (Hosea 11:3,4)

Bless us with generosity, Holy Spirit.

In Prayer and Peace

According to Richard Dahlstrom in *O2: Breathing New Life Into Faith,* we're "largely numb to the revelation of glory coming to us through creation. And yet in the Bible this created world has been a vital means of God's self revelation."

Get outside. Take walks. Garden. Watch a flock winging its way across the sky. Learn to identify birds, animals. Enjoy the moon's waxing and waning; planets, too.

Walk barefoot on a beach. Feel the cool dampness, the hot dry graininess. Hear the water slap against the shore. Follow the antics of gulls and other sea creatures.

Learn to read the hoof and paw prints in your garden or on fresh snow. Enjoy squirrels' play; chipmunks' stripes; raccoons' amazing dexterity; bees' industriousness.

To revel in Earth and its creatures is to revel in their Author and Sustainer and ours!

You stretch out the heavens....You set the earth on its foundation, so that it shall never be shaken. (Psalm 104:2,5)

Help us know and appreciate Your self revelation in Creation, God.

Good Deeds Go a Long Way

When Tyler Page saw a report about Ghanaian children being sold by their parents for food, he immediately wanted to do something. He told his mother, Laura, that he wanted to raise $240 to keep one child safe for a year. Kids Helping Kids-Project Ghana was born.

Page encouraged others to pitch in. He raised money with things kids could do: car washes, garage sales and lemonade stands. From there, the project only grew bigger; they eventually raised $38,000.

"I'll never again underestimate what kids are capable of achieving," said Tyler Page.

It only takes a simple act of generosity, or even a couple of car washes, to raise funds for needy children. How can you respectfully, gently, encourage a child's generosity?

Godliness is valuable in every way, holding promise for both the present life and the life to come. (1 Timothy 4:8)

Help parents respectfully and gently encourage their children's generosity, Gentle Jesus.

The New York that Was

The corner of Bayard and Mulberry Streets in Manhattan's Chinatown is known as "The Bend," due to Mulberry Street's prominent curve.

Today, The Bend is a bustling, vibrant convergence of restaurants, bakeries and fish markets. Hard to believe that in the 1870s, the area was the epicenter of what some called the worst slum in New York. The famed journalist, photographer and social reformer Jacob Riis once described it as a "vast, human pig-sty."

Riis had an uncanny ability to translate personal interviews with hundreds of impoverished Bend residents into compelling statistics and images. For example, Riis told of 12 people sleeping in a single room that measured 13 square feet, and paying five cents a night for the privilege.

How well do you know your city, the good, the bad and the ugly? To learn these histories is to put down deep roots and to build connectedness.

The beginning of wisdom is the most sincere desire for instruction. (Wisdom of Solomon 6:17)

Encourage our efforts to grow roots, Ancient of Days.

S-T-U-F-F in your Home

So you want to let go of the stuff that clogs your home, not to mention your life. How to begin? According to *Family Circle* magazine you'll need to accomplish these tasks:

Overcome obstacles. Ask "does this serve my vision?"

Commit time. They suggest 20 minutes and two garbage bags a day, every day

Communicate with your children. Help them know the benefits of being organized; lay the foundation for a clutter-free life

Change the role stuff plays in your life and the lives of your children.

Don't hold on to clutter. Your *present* life is your priority, not the past or the future.

Learn to let go!

Celebrate the calm and space you now enjoy.

A Goodwill store, the Salvation Army or a St. Vincent DePaul shop will benefit, too.

Life does not consist in the abundance of possessions. (Luke 12:16)

Give families the courage to rid their homes of clutter, God.

Meeting Mickey Mouse

Growing up in Lincoln, Nebraska, Yankee pitcher Joba Chamberlain never went to Disney World. His father, Harlan, could not afford a family vacation. So on his first visit to the land of Mickey Mouse as an adult, he decided to give someone else the opportunity he hadn't had.

"I wanted to do something for a family that doesn't have enough extra money to do something they want to do," Chamberlain explains.

He traded text messages with his former school coach, asking him to suggest a student. Fifth grader Kristan Martin was selected, and, with his parents, brother and sister, joined the Yankees player on the Florida journey.

"Baseball is going to be over, and I want people to know that I was a good baseball player, but a better person," explains Chamberlain.

Our actions, no matter the playing field, should seek to enrich the lives of those around us.

Always seek to do good. (1 Thessalonians 5:15)

Give me the grace to share my blessings, Spirit of Joy.

Spiritual Enlightenment in Daily Chores?

It's probably safe to say that most of us find the drudgery of housecleaning anything but inspiring. But are we missing something?

According to writer Akiko Busch, the routine predictability of housekeeping can impart a sense of comfort and consistency. "The solace of continuity imposes some symmetry on domestic life," writes Busch. What's more, in a world where one's sense of security can be shattered in an instant through illness, accident or death, ordinary tasks may help "establish a bedrock for the seismic changes that can so easily follow," Busch continues.

In performing routine tasks each day, our lives gain structure and the hope that what we hold sacred will remain intact, even if just for a little longer.

Instead of dreading your daily routines, try viewing them as gifts of security, predictability and consistency.

In returning and rest you shall be saved; in quietness and in trust shall be your strength. (Isaiah 30:15)

Thank you, Lord and Savior, for the gift of life.

Within a Caring Community

When Frank King was deployed to Iraq, his wife, Lisa, worried about how she'd care for their five children and help them through days of missing their dad.

Lori Schultz wondered how she'd survive with both her husband James and her 24-year-old daughter Heidi in Iraq.

Both of these Hastings, Minnesota, women found help right in their own backyard.

King received backpacks of school supplies for her three eldest thanks to Minnesota Veteran Family Support. Schultz's friends and neighbors pitched in to help her and her two teenage sons. "They'd fix dinner and make repairs around the house," she says. "Little things like that really mean a lot."

What are the needs of your neighbors? Look around. Lend a hand.

Do not be hard-hearted or tight-fisted toward your needy neighbor. ...Open your hand, willingly. ...Do not entertain a mean thought. ...Give liberally and be ungrudging.
(Deuteronomy 15:7,8,9,10)

Help me to love my neighbor, Father, just as You love me.

Teacher, Laborer, Brain Surgeon

Two decades ago, the hands of this brain surgeon were those of a teacher, a farm worker, a manual laborer, a student.

A Mexican native and naturalized American, Dr. Q as he's called, remembers childhood nights when there was no food. His father said, "If you want to be like me don't go to school." He listened, graduated college and taught school in Mexico.

But because "as long as there's poverty, humans will always seek out a better way to live," he came to the U.S. and became a farm worker. After a year he got another job and went to night community college. Norm Nichols, the speech and debate coach at San Joaquin Delta Community College took Alfredo Quiñones-Hinojosa into his family and mentored him.

Eventually Alfredo Quinones-Hinojosa graduated cum laude from Harvard Medical School. Today, he is a renowned brain surgeon and researcher. "Give the world your best," Dr. Quinones-Hinojosa says. Yes, give it your best. And, recognize others' efforts to give the world their best.

Honor physicians...their gift of healing comes from the Most High. (Sirach 38:1,2)

Help us respect naturalized citizens' intelligence, God.

Music to My Ears

If you're a music lover, then you'll be happy to know that listening is good for you. "Cutting-edge research reveals how music can help you ease pain, think smarter, feel energized, and fight disease," notes Jordan Lite in *Prevention* Magazine.

- In pain? Combine music and guided imagery. "Music seems to stimulate the release of pain-masking endorphins," according to a music therapy professor.

- Trouble breathing? Try singing or playing a wind instrument to relax while increasing your breathing capacity.

- Can't sleep? Make music part of your daily sleep ritual.

- Depressed? Experts recommend listening to up-tempo music undisturbed for 10 to 20 minutes.

All these potential benefits and more from something you already enjoy no doubt leaves you feeling this is "music to your ears."

Praise God...with trumpet...lute and harp...with tambourine and dance...with strings and pipe... with clanging (and)...loud clashing cymbals! (Psalm 150:1,3,4,5)

Thanks for the gift of music, Creator.

Going Green — Literally

Today, people are so busy it's a struggle to stay in touch with loved ones, never mind Mother Earth. Yet the more disconnected we become from nature, the more disconnected we are from ourselves. Gardening can be a perfect remedy.

Writer Gerri Hirshey admits that she's been "afflicted since childhood" with the gardening bug. She treasures a garden's small, domestic miracles, such as when her son tastes her home grown produce. He can tell the difference between store-bought and "Mom broccoli."

Each Spring she and her husband turn over the soil and discover the soft, "wormy black gold that hove up beneath the winter debris." She recalls watering seedlings, only to have a ruby-throated hummingbird fly in to enjoy the spray.

What a lovely way to view God's earth, the home we share with all the creatures. When did you last literally connect with the Earth and its other inhabitants?

How great is the house of God, how vast the territory that He possesses! (Baruch 3:24)

Thank You, Gracious Creator, for this world's wonders.

Now I Hear You

While still in college, Bill Austin heard an inner calling, changed his studies, and went on to a long career helping others improve their hearing.

"In a single day, I decided to change my life," said Austin.

Austin had planned to study medicine but while working for a hearing aid company he watched in amazement as a youngster's face lit up once the child had been fitted with hearing aids. Described by *People* magazine as a hearing-aid mogul, the Missouri native is founder and CEO of Starkey Laboratories. His clientele has included a president, an actor, a beauty queen and other famous people. But Austin finds the most reward in giving hearing aids to hundreds of thousands of unknown youngsters through his Starkey Hearing Foundation.

In the hustle and bustle of daily life, make time to stop and listen. What do you hear?

Keep silence and hear...obey the Lord your God, observing His commandments and His statutes. (Deuteronomy 27:9,10)

Holy Spirit, open my ears and eyes, my mind and soul. Help me respond in love and with love.

Building History

Author Richard Wright and inventor George Washington Carver slept there. Paul Robeson was discovered on its stage, and Jackie Robinson coached basketball in the gym.

Rich in such black history, the Harlem Y.M.C.A. continues to do what it has always done—serve a community. Today that means offering mambo, salsa, belly dancing, and yoga classes. There's also a New American Welcome Center, where immigrants can learn English and become familiar with their adopted country.

There are plans to move to a larger space to accommodate a charter school and a large kitchen for classes on healthy cooking, an effort to curb the area's high rates of obesity and diabetes.

Until then, the 11-story brick building stands as an homage to the past, hope for today, and promise for the future.

May we, too, always respect our past, treasure our present and labor for a better tomorrow.

Lord, You have been our dwelling place in all generations...from everlasting to everlasting You are God. (Psalm 90:1,2)

Yesterday, today and tomorrow, You, God, are our Lover.

Opening the World of Language to Others

Daan Chen was 11, when he immigrated to the United States from China. "It was hard to communicate," he recalls. "My English teacher gave me a dictionary, and every day I checked all the words I could."

Today, Chen eases others' transition: a high-school senior, he teaches younger, academically at risk high-school students how to navigate their English-Chinese dictionaries. He finds great satisfaction in watching them move closer to graduating high-school and beginning college. He advises, "Get with a group of people that build you up, not break you down."

And apparently, he has taken his own advice to heart. Chen was recently accepted at a large university.

Hard work can help us overcome obstacles, but usually we need others' help to triumph. When the going gets tough, reach for a helping hand.

I will give you my support. (2 Samuel 3:12)

Remind me that I cannot thrive alone, God.

A World-Class Winner

Barbara Buchan may answer questions more slowly than many people, but when it comes to cycling, few are faster than she.

Buchan, the oldest member of the United States Paralympic Team, broke the world record in the individual 3,000 meter cycling pursuit and took home a gold medal for her accomplishment.

The win came 26 years after Buchan had a near-fatal bicycle accident that left her comatose for two months. Although the accident resulted in permanent brain injuries including diminished brain function and cognitive problems as well as serious physical challenges, Buchan's philosophy prevented her from focusing on the past.

"You can be very upset at the world and have everyone take care of you," says Buchan, "or, you can get back on your feet again."

How do you view your life's setbacks? As the ends, or as the beginning of something new?

Happy are those...who have not given up their hope. (Sirach 14:2)

Prince of Peace, infuse me with optimism.

Understanding Life on the Gulf

Hurricane Katrina devastated the Gulf Coast in 2005, leveling entire communities and literally washing away the residents' lives. Many people fled the storm. Do you ever wonder why some stayed?

When volunteers from two New Hampshire churches traveled to Mississippi to help rebuild homes, they learned that the reason many residents decided to risk their lives and weather the storm was quite simple. Having endured lifetimes of hurricanes, some residents felt familiar enough with them to take their chances. Others were afraid to leave precious belongings.

The volunteers found one common thread among all of the storm survivors: they were eager to talk about their experience and how the storm has affected their lives.

Sometimes, a listening ear is the kindest gift you can offer someone. By listening, you are sharing in another's life, helping to ease their pain.

O afflicted one, storm-tossed, and not comforted... in righteousness you shall be established...far from oppression...and from terror. (Isaiah 54:11,14)

Comfort the lonely, Merciful Savior.

Wagons Ho!

Time seemed to turn back 100 years, except for the rubber tires, bucket seats and seatbelts. The modifications to the old wooden wagon, pulled by two mules, were made to help it lead a wagon train on a 240-mile trek across the rugged plains of South Dakota to Deadwood.

The 17-day trip from Fort Pierre in 2008 marked the 100th anniversary of the last wagon train to travel that route to the gold in the Black Hills of South Dakota. Fifty-four wagons, pulled by horses, mules and oxen, began the anniversary ride. They were accompanied by 225 people on horseback.

"It will bring back some of the old days," said one rider, drawn to the event by the lure of the open range and the history of the route.

Life's journey forward is helped by a look back at the lessons of the past.

O Lord, I have heard of Your renown, and I stand in awe, O Lord, of Your work. (Habakkuk 3:2)

Guide our steps today, Abba. Grant us safe travels.

Building a Model for the Future

Dr. Eugene Newport, a veteran community planner and visiting fellow at the Massachusetts Institute of Technology is familiar with disaster sites, having seen war zones firsthand.

Yet when he visited New Orleans in late 2007, a full two years after Hurricane Katrina had devastated the area, he said sadly "I have never seen such devastation."

Newport was horrified to find that people displaced as by Hurricane Katrina were not back in their homes. He cited a combination of government failure, racism and poor public policy among the causes.

So Dr. Newport and the Episcopal Diocese of Louisiana formed coalitions to help youth, improve public education and rebuild homes for people adversely affected by the hurricane. We "feel that our project could be used as a model for the country," says Newport.

Hope is hard to muster in the most desperate of situations. Yet, that's when it's most needed.

The Lord God...will gather the lambs in His arms, and carry them in His bosom, and gently lead the mother sheep. (Isaiah 40:10,11)

Jesus our Good Shepherd, give me the strength to be hopeful in hopeless circumstances.

The Teenager Who Built a School

Carly Zalenski starting helping others when she was eight. The Ohio youngster helped hand out Thanksgiving baskets to families in need. The next year, Carly went door-to-door asking for used coats, hats, gloves and scarves to distribute with those baskets.

But Carly wanted to do more—to "change lives," she says. She remembered hearing about how her grandmother's Rotary Club built a school in Vietnam. She would too, she decided.

At 12, she made her first fund-raising speech. Two years and many speeches and fundraising events later, Carly had raised $50,000, a sum matched by the Vietnam Children's Fund. Soon she found herself standing in Ho Chi Minh City at the dedication of a school she knew would make a difference.

Needs—big and small—are all around us. It's up to each of us to light one candle of hope at a time.

The fruit of the righteous is a tree of life. (Proverbs 11:30)

Show me how I can give hope today in Your name, Master.

Getting Through Grief

Dealing with the death of a loved one is difficult on many levels, but coping with the emotions is the toughest part according to Jessie Flynn, founder of the Center for Living in Metuchen, New Jersey.

Fear is one issue. "As soon as you go into the future, it's going to raise anxiety," she explains. Write down your concerns and seek people and resources to help you. Loneliness is also painful. Yet, Flynn believes it can also be a gift. "If you can sit in that lonely, quiet time, it can become a very spiritual thing."

Finally, Flynn adds, "Grief is exhausting stuff. It takes energy and it takes other people. Day by day, you re-create your life. We never say good-bye. What you are doing is changing the relationship from a physical one to a spiritual connection."

Encourage grieving people to take their time and to be gentle with themselves. And be sure to pray as well.

God...consoles us in all our affliction, so that we may be able to console those who are in any affliction. (2 Corinthians 1:3,4)

Merciful Lord, help me hold tight to You and to help others in pain to do the same.

A Match Made in Heaven

Most teachers would say that sharing knowledge with their students is part of the job. But sharing life itself? That takes a special teacher indeed.

Patricia Donahue, an elementary school teacher in New Lenox, Illinois, discovered that one of her fourth grade students had polycystic kidney disease and was in need of a transplant. Brandon Shafer's own family was unable to make the appropriate match. That's when Donahue, a first year teacher, offered to be tested and learned she was a perfect match.

Donahue was inspired by the fact that her own father had benefited from a bone marrow transplant when he was diagnosed with leukemia. The successful surgery was performed in 2006 and the teacher and her former student have developed a close bond since then.

Sometimes we are called on to do extraordinary things. And what we do can make all the difference in the world.

Do not neglect to do good and to share what you have. (Hebrews 13:16)

Holy Savior, bless our efforts to assist people most in need of help.

Music-Filled Skies

On September 11, 2001, New Yorker Haruko Smith was in Paris on business. "I came back to a very different New York," explains the Tokyo-born businesswoman, "and I had an urgent feeling: I have to do something."

Her vision: for one day, wrap the world in music. "Instead of more negativity, let's celebrate this day as a remembrance," Smith observes. She adds that "A communication about peace can best be done by music."

Smith's first September concert took place on September 11, 2002. Today it's a global phenomenon, bringing free music in all genres to a number of locations in New York, as well as to more than 80 other American and international cities on that same day each year.

When faced with unexplainable tragedy, our own or another's, create goodness and light to dispel the darkness.

Why are you cast down, O my soul, and why are you disquieted within me? Hope in God; for I shall again praise Him, my help. (Psalm 42:5)

From the depths of my sorrow, I courageously raise my head up, knowing I'm never far from Your gaze, Lord.

Lifetime's Work, Struggle Recognized

For much of his life, physicist and cosmologist (philosophers who study the origin and structure of the universe) Father Michal Heller conducted complex research on spirituality and the origins of the universe under the Communist government in Poland.

Internationally recognized, Heller has written more than 30 books and nearly 400 papers on topics such as the unification of general relativity and quantum mechanics. But what is perhaps most significant is that Heller successfully injected Christianity into his work.

Heller's courage and efforts were recognized in 2008, when he was awarded the prestigious Templeton Prize, the world's largest annual monetary award to an individual, for progress toward research or discoveries about spiritual realities.

When life seems difficult, imagine your life without civil liberties or freedom of religion.

For freedom Christ has set us free...do not submit again to slavery. (Galatians 5:1)

Remind me, God, that the freedom I want for myself must be the freedom I want even for those with whom I disagree.

Your Life, Your Work

Your life needs balance. But only you, not your employer or anyone else, can achieve it. Here are suggestions from Victor M. Parachin writing in *Liguorian* magazine:

- Shape how you work. Take and keep charge of your career.
- Keep a Sabbath. Do not work 24/7 for yourself or an employer.
- Pray. Daily. In your own words and/or memorized ones. Wherever and whenever you can.
- Pause before taking on additional responsibilities. Be alert to over-commitment.
- List priorities for your life. Check off items as you achieve them.
- Begin to live your balanced life now. It'll get more balanced over time.

The poet William Wordsworth wrote, "Getting and spending, we lay waste our powers." Aim, instead, for harmony.

> **What gain have the workers from their toil?...There is nothing better for them than to be happy and enjoy themselves.**
> **(Ecclesiastes 3:9,12)**

Keep Your truth, Your freedom, Your justice fresh in our minds, Holy Wisdom.

Bringing Hope, and Learning, Too

Twenty-two year old Malbri Reyes from New Jersey could have spent her summer enjoying leisure activities, like many of her peers. Instead, Reyes joined a group of students to bring hope to those in need.

As coordinated by the Catholic Center at Rutgers University, Reyes and 15 others traveled to Tanzania to bring hope to the HIV/AIDS orphans; students at a vocational high school; and children, disabled adults and the elderly at a home run by the Missionaries of Charity.

"The children are living a lot longer," because of the care received says Reyes, of the orphans at the hospice.

The volunteers brought U.S. culture and received lessons in African culture in return. While the group's aim was to serve as Jesus would serve, Reyes says, she learned to slow down and take everything in; to enjoy life more; and to make time for people.

This is my prayer, that your love may overflow more and more with knowledge and full insight to help you to determine what is best. (Philippians 1:9-10)

Jesus, help us learn from other cultures and peoples what's genuinely important.

Garden-Fresh School Lunches !?

Mention the phrase "school lunch" and few will conjure up images of a well-balanced meal with fresh veggies and fruits.

St. Michael's Episcopal Day School in California wants to change that. Thanks to the initiative of a school parent and the headmaster, the school created an on-site garden that feeds the students.

Through the parents' ongoing fundraising efforts and hands-on labor, the garden provides snap peas, strawberries and fresh produce for the school's lunches.

The idea is catching on elsewhere, too. The cafeteria at St. Philip's Academy in Newark, New Jersey, functions as a nutrition center as well as an open kitchen. Cooking classes help teach students healthful eating habits, and parents receive newsletters promoting healthful dietary habits beyond lunch.

If our bodies need nourishment to stay healthy, so do our souls. How do you feed your soul?

Jesus...said...“Come away to a deserted place all by yourselves and rest a while.”
(Mark 6:30,31)

Messiah, teach us to go apart, to enter into silence, to rest and so to feed our souls.

A Rockin' Rosh Hashana

Rosh Hashana, the Jewish New Year, is a time of celebration and joy with the traditional singing of the Torah and the chanting of prayers.

One congregation, however, celebrates Rosh Hashana differently. The Shul of New York celebrated the New Year with the folk rock music of The Shul Band, a self-described rock and klezmer band that includes Jewish and non-Jewish members of mixed ethnicities.

While the departure from tradition may shock some, others appreciate it. A member of the congregation says, "It's like a revival meeting" and when The Shul Band plays, "I find it hard to stay in my seat."

Congregants enjoy the multi-cultural band and the inclusive stage it sets. One of the musicians says, "It's a symbol of what this progressive and welcoming congregation is all about."

Lives and experiences are enriched by diversity. How can you foster diversity within your community, workplace, and family?

In the seventh month, on the first day...you shall observe a day of complete rest....you shall not work...and you shall present the Lord's offering by fire. (Leviticus 23:24,25)

Open our hearts, Creator, to our common humanity, to what binds us each to the other.

Beyond Mere Vision

Michael Hingson was born blind. But that never stopped him. He earned a Master's degree in physics, married, and, by 2001, he was a regional manager for a corporation in New York's World Trade Center.

Then, September 11, 2001 occurred. Hingson escaped his North Tower office thanks to his guide dog, Roselle, who traveled everywhere with him.

"We were only about 100 meters from the parking lot when the South Tower collapsed," he recalls. He fearfully wondered, "God, did you take us out of one building to have us perish on the streets below?"

Hingson and Roselle ran for safety. Surviving has changed his life. Hingson changed careers and now devotes his talents and efforts to the work of the Guide Dogs Association.

Tragedy can give rise to triumph. Our survival as a nation depends on our ability to rise above tragedy and work together as one people.

Have unity of spirit. (1 Peter 3:8)

Heal our nation and our people, Great God.

The Last Time

None of us can see into the future and part of the zest of living comes from life's unexpected surprises. Some, however, are anything but happy. Tragedies can in fact strike without warning.

An anonymous author penned the poem, excerpted below, in response to September 11, 2001:

If I knew it would be the last time that I'd see you fall asleep,

I would tuck you in more tightly

and pray the Lord, your soul to keep.

If I knew it would be the last time that I'd see you walk out the door, I'd give you a hug and a kiss,

And call you back for more.

So hold your loved ones close today and whisper in their ears,

How much you love them, and that you'll hold them dear.

Live in the present. It's all we really have.

God is our refuge and strength, a very present help in trouble. Therefore we will not fear. (Psalm 46:1-2)

Jesus, calm my anxieties, and help me enjoy each moment of this life the Father has given me.

Real-Life Courage

When Sidney Poitier won the 1964 Academy Award for Best Actor for his work in *Lilies of the Field*, he was the first black man to win the Oscar. Yet what lies behind his public persona eclipses his popular fame and accomplishments.

Poitier spent his first ten years on Cat Island, The Bahamas. He had his first encounters with racism in Nassau and then in Florida. He moved to Harlem. Because he could read at only a fourth-grade level, he struggled to get theatre jobs. Eventually, through the help of a Jewish waiter and by listening to the radio, he learned how to read and lost his Bahamian accent. Soon, his career in theatre, and eventually films, flourished.

Faith, courage and perseverance enabled Poitier to overcome obstacles and achieve great things.

How do you react when life is at its most difficult?

Happy are those who persevere. (Daniel 12:12)

Refresh my courage, Blessed Trinity.

The Leader Who Follows

Are you a leader? People shy away from the word, knowing that leaders are usually famous and rich, always powerful and too often arrogant.

In fact, genuine leaders are first servants and followers. Here's what Rev. Todd Krygsheld of Holland, Michigan's Ebenezer Reformed Church says about leadership and Jesus:

"The New Testament reveals that *followership* precedes leadership, revealing Jesus as the ultimate example of *followership*. With His *not-My-will-but-Your-will-be-done* heart, Jesus followed His Father's will perfectly—even humbling himself and becoming obedient to death.

"He knew that in order for His disciples to be leaders they first needed to be followers. Before they ever led, they followed Jesus, watched Jesus, listened to Jesus, and were taught by Jesus. …Leadership if not something we go into but rather grow into as we follow Christ more fully."

Seek God's will. Be ready to lead.

(Jesus) went down with them...to Nazareth, and was obedient to (Joseph and Mary). His mother treasured all these things in her heart. And Jesus increased in wisdom and in years. (Luke 2:51-52)

Holy Spirit, guide me in doing the Father's will with every fiber of my being.

Taking Your Time

As schedules fill up and "must-do" tasks multiply, the time to enjoy life seems in ever shorter supply.

While taking care of older relatives, Susan Orshan decided to make time for herself with an early morning walk. "It helped me to focus on my day," she says. "I returned home feeling great because I started the day doing something good for me."

Setting priorities for your day also helps. What's more important: a kitchen floor clean enough to eat off, or time with family and/or friends?

And remember that you can't, and don't have to, do everything. Sharing tasks helps everyone to get to what they enjoy sooner.

In the end, remember that God's timeless, ageless love for us should compel us always to seek for ourselves and others what God seeks—the very best for each of us.

Better is a handful with quiet than two handfuls with toil, and a chasing after wind. (Ecclesiastes 4:6)

Creator, reveal Your wisdom to me that I may always choose Your path.

Brick by Brick, Changing Lives

Volunteers who participate in St. Francis Builds, a part of Habitat for Humanity, are changing lives, one brick at a time.

Launched from a Silver Spring, Maryland, Franciscan parish, the group enlists volunteers to help build homes in impoverished areas globally.

Olinda Ojeda Villegas and her husband, José Simon Illanes were taken aback by the Americans' generosity, kindness and work ethic and surprised to learn that the volunteers paid their own way to Bolivia. "We all fear what is unknown, right?" admits Ojeda. "But they were very kind and caring. They helped us with everything; we got used to them."

In a week, the Americans helped build the foundation and walls of Ojeda's house.

Treat every man, woman and child of every religion, nationality, race, gender, language, or political persuasion the way you would want them to treat you.

How can you say to your neighbor, "Friend, let me take out the speck in your eye," when you yourself do not see the log in your own eye? (Luke 6:42)

Remind us that ours is a nation of immigrants and their descendants, Prince of Peace.

Broken Pieces to a Beautiful Picture

In a recent survey, the Citizens Committee for Youth in New York City rated the Mott Haven section of the Bronx the city's worst neighborhood in which to raise a child. It observed that the area is plagued by violence, drugs and a lack of resources.

But artist-educator Kim Iacono set out to provide a colorful example of all that's good about the neighborhood. She created a "Harmony Mosaic" depicting the four elements: earth, air, fire and water as an outdoor artwork based on the drawings and ideas of her students.

"I wanted them to see that they can do beautiful things regardless of the circumstances around them," she says.

When problems plague our own life, we need always to hold on to the light that is from within us.

**The Spirit helps us in our weakness.
(Romans 8:26)**

Come, Holy Spirit, with Your life-giving light and love.

Supporting Life

Heidi Murkoff wrote *Baby Basics* and *What to Expect When You're Expecting* to remind women to stay healthy during pregnancy; to help them understand any complications, and make wise medical decisions.

Unfortunately, these books are not readily accessible to the more than one million poor mothers-to-be in the U.S. each year. So Murkoff created the What to Expect Foundation to help these women make informed medical choices. Volunteers even teach these women how to read. And Mom's Clubs are specifically designed to assist pregnant teens.

In whatever way you can, help poor pregnant women and teens have healthy pregnancies, safe deliveries and thriving babies. But don't stop there. Support human life from the womb to the grave. Make the extra effort.

It was You who took me from the womb; You kept me safe on my mother's breast. On You I was cast from my birth. (Psalm 22:9-10)

God who knits us up in the womb, remind us to support all life: infants, children, teens, adults, the aged.

A Heart Full of Prayer

Each of us needs to learn to pray first with our hearts. There's a story told about a rabbi to whom an angel appeared, telling him to visit a poor farmer whose prayers "had reached the highest heavens."

The rabbi asked the farmer how he prayed. "I cannot pray," said the farmer. "All I know are the first nine letters of the alphabet."

The rabbi asked him what he did on Yom Kippur, the Day of Atonement.

"I went to the synagogue and saw how intently everyone was praying and my heart broke," said the farmer. "So I recited the letters I know of the alphabet. I said, 'Dear God, take these letters and form them into prayers that will rise up like the scent of honeysuckle, the most beautiful scent I know.' And I said that with all my strength, over and over."

Then the rabbi understood the prayer of the heart.

Our Father in heaven, hallowed be Your name. Your kingdom come. Your will be done, on earth as it is in heaven. Give us this day our daily bread. And forgive us our debts, as we also have forgiven our debtors.
(Matthew 6:9-12)

Teach me how to pray, my Lord.

Through the Labyrinth

Ptolemy Tompkins, editor of *Guideposts* magazine, writes of "moving deeper and deeper into the twisting green interior" of the boxwood labyrinth in Washington, D.C.'s Montrose Park as a child. He "felt the world fade away" and knew something was waiting for him "at the heart of the maze." While it was "a little scary," the mystery, excitement and fear made the world outside feel "a little bit larger."

Tompkins remembered this when he walked a labyrinth. Since "there are no walls you just follow the path at your feet." And since there are no "wrong turns," you cannot lose your way.

Life can be a labyrinth with barriers, wrong turns, darkness; challenges, tragedies and disappointments. Ask God to lead you in His righteousness and make His way plain so that you can walk in safety.

Lead me, O Lord, in Your righteousness because of my enemies; make Your way straight before me. (Psalm 5:8)

Good Shepherd, lead me.

In These Tough Economic Times

Here are ideas to help you cope with financial problems:

Stay optimistic. Do one thing a day for your community, your family, your spirit, your home, your job.

See the big picture. Remember what's important: love, family and friends. Choose to be happy.

Enjoy inexpensive entertainment. Try a game night. Rent movies. Read books from the library.

Cook for yourself and those you love. Try to do so on a shoestring budget.

Go into 'survival mode' if necessary. Get a second job. Shop at dollar stores. List items for sale on eBay or Craigslist.

Enjoy quality time outdoors. Take a walk. Picnic on your lawn or in a park.

Give to those who have even less. Work at a food pantry, soup kitchen or a second hand clothing store.

We are rich. We just need to be aware of it.

(May) your love...overflow...with knowledge and full insight to help you to determine what is best. (Philippians 1:9-10)

Abba, help us appreciate how wealthy we are, least of all in material possessions.

Messages from Home

While more and more people use e-mail to communicate with family and friends as well as for business purposes, there's still something special about opening your mailbox and finding a personal letter or card awaiting you.

When Meredith Mayes of Jersey City, New Jersey, was in college far from home, she always looked forward to receiving a card or note from her grandmother on a regular basis. Sometimes they were brief, other times, chatty. They might be funny or sentimental, but the notes kept coming— 300 of them over the years Mayes attended college.

Mayes is sure of the number because she saved and still treasures every single one of them.

We have so many opportunities to affect the lives of others if we just make the effort to reach out in love.

Love your enemies, do good...expecting nothing in return. (Luke 6:35)

Blessed Trinity, open my mind and heart and grant me the desire to seek to serve Your people in any way I can.

The Pollution Police

When Juan Hernandez moved to West Oakland from Bakersfield, California, his asthma flared up.

To help the high school student find out why, a teacher sent him on a "toxic tour" of the neighborhood. The reasons were everywhere—four freeways, a metal recycling plant and an aluminum smelting facility.

"I said to myself, 'I'm living in this place that has some of the worst pollution in all of Oakland, and I've got to do something about it,'" Hernandez recalls.

He did. With support from the state and environmental organizations, Hernandez and his classmates tested the air outside their school. Finding elevated levels of heavy metals, they held a press conference and grabbed the attention of neighbors, elected officials and even the scrap plant, which has since cleaned up.

Never be afraid to stand up for what's right.

Be very steadfast to observe and do all that is written in the book of the Law of Moses. (Joshua 23:6)

Lord, grant me wisdom, determination and courage.

Survival 101 for 20 Somethings

Gen Y-ers like every generation have to learn what it means to be a mature adult, despite difficult times. Just how do you survive your twenties? Christine Hassler, author of *20-Something, 20-Everything,* has some suggestions:

- Start finding yourself. Open a self-help book.
- Be yourself.
- Find your balance between type A and type B.
- Prioritize your goals.
- Know the difference between independence and stubbornness.
- Cultivate your physical, emotional and spiritual health.
- Be grateful. You have many blessings.
- Establish your spending habits.
- Know what you want out of your job.

Remember that you are not alone.

Remember your Creator in the days of your youth. (Ecclesiastes 12:1)

Bless young adults just starting out on their life's adventure, Christ our Redeemer.

10 Legs, 4,800 Books — and More!

As a young teacher, Luis Soriano recognized reading's power. So, he loaded Alfa and Beto, his burros, with 70 books and visited neighbors around his town of La Gloria, Colombia. Groups of children waited to hear him read to them. Biblioburro was born!

When he heard *The Ballad of Maria Abdala* read by its author Juan Gossaín on the radio, he wrote Gossaín asking for a copy. In return, Gossaín detailed Soriano's project on his radio program. Books poured in. He now has over 4,800!

A decade later Biblioburro has become an institution. Every weekend Soriano brings books to those who don't have any.

To supplement his teacher's salary, Soriano and his wife Diana also run a restaurant where diners engage in current events discussions.

Soriano began Biblioburro to connect isolated children and adults with the outside world. How can you connect with others?

When He was twelve years old...the boy Jesus stayed behind...in the temple, sitting among the teachers, listening to them and asking them questions. (Luke 2:42,43,46)

Jesus, help me open the world of books to at least one child or adult.

"We Shall Overcome Someday"

Tennessee's Highlander Folk School was launched in 1932 in an area devastated by deforestation, closed mines, subsistence farming and widespread poverty. It recognized the ability of local people to determine their own fate.

The school's first focus was on labor, farmer and Appalachian rights, but, by 1953 it was active in desegregation efforts. In fact, The Highlander Folk School wrote the first curriculum in the South to prepare teachers and community members for desegregation. Rosa Parks' remarked on her 1955 interracial residential experience at the school that "we all were treated equally and without any tension."

Local governments forced the closing of the school in 1961. But it was reborn as the Highlander Research and Education Center first in Knoxville, where it focuses on social justice issues.

The struggle for human rights continues around the world. Promote justice for all.

Act with justice and righteousness, and deliver from the...oppressor anyone who has been robbed. And do no wrong or violence to the alien, the orphan, and the widow, or shed innocent blood. (Jeremiah 22:3)

Precious Lord, remind us that unless all have equal rights and justice, none have them.

Simple Pottery, Saved Lives

Bronx-born inventor and volunteer Ron Rivera likened his ceramic water filters to "weapons of biological mass destruction." And in a way, that is what they were.

For 25 years, Rivera went to the poorest villages of Latin America, Africa and Asia, teaching local potters to fashion an ingenious water-purifying device out of terra-cotta. A recent study in Cambodia found that Rivera's filters cut the incidence of diarrhea (the leading cause of death in the third world) in half. Rivera said, "you put dirty water in, gray water that many communities still drink, and it comes out crystal clear."

Rivera himself died from a dangerous form of malaria while establishing a water-filter factory in Nigeria.

Service can involve risk, even danger, but mostly it means putting one's own needs aside so as to help others. How far are you willing to go to serve others in Jesus' name?

I was thirsty and you gave Me something to drink. (Matthew 25:35)

How can we help slake the world's thirst, Holy Savior?

Playing the Game

There's a saying that winning isn't everything, it's the only thing. But in both sports and in life, there really is more to it.

Back in 1925, golfing legend Bobby Jones penalized himself a stroke for something no one else saw: his ball moved a bit in the rough and his iron touched it. That penalty caused Jones to tie with Willie McFarlane who went on to win the playoff.

Something similar happened in 1978 during the Hall of Fame Classic when Tom Kite's self-imposed stroke cost him the tournament.

In both cases, reporters later asked the players why they had done what they had. And in both cases the answers were essentially the same: "There's only one way to play the game."

Winning can be a wonderful thing. But, upholding your values is even better.

To (God) you shall hold fast...He is your praise; He is your God. (Deuteronomy 10:20,21)

Spirit of Truth, shape my conscience according to the Commandments to love God and to love my neighbors as I love myself.

Financial Woes Raise Concerns, Eyebrows

The on-going economic crisis has swept far and wide, as everyday people around the globe watch their assets plummet in the wake of financial markets' collapse. This has brought long overdue scrutiny to the practices of many financial institutions.

For example, the Internal Revenue Service recently participated in a broad federal inquiry into the offshore banking accounts of UBS, the world's largest private bank. They were seeking to identify individuals who were hiding assets in foreign accounts to avoid paying taxes. It's estimated that upwards of 19,000 clients may have evaded $300 million a year in taxes.

Taxes are no fun to pay, but pay them, we must. Taxes help finance our local, state and national governments; help support the unemployed and aged; and provide money for infrastructure repair and maintenance.

"Teacher...is it lawful to pay taxes to the emperor, or not?"..."Give therefore to the emperor the things that are the emperor's." (Matthew 16,17,21)

God, remind us to take our responsibilities as citizens seriously.

The Spirit of Community

What we see as easy household and yard chores may not be so easy for others. But with help, good will and inspiration from Mount St. Mary High School and the College Hill Neighborhood Association, life is a lot easier for many people in Oklahoma City.

Two Christian Service Days were dedicated to helping neighbors around the school. Household projects such as mowing lawns, raking leaves, pulling weeds, cleaning windows and other small projects were carried out by students and sponsors.

"As our future leaders, it is important for our students to get involved in civic engagement and Christian service," said Ned Berghausen, Christian Service coordinator. "We live out our Christian faith by serving others. Our mission at the Mount is to live lives of service."

How do you live out your faith? A small act of kindness can go a long way in assisting neighbors in need.

Lay up your treasure according to the commandments of the Most High. (Sirach 29:11)

Divine Lord, may good deeds done for others be my true treasure.

Education One Day at a Time

Do you wish you could continue your education or keep up with current ideas from the best schools?

If you're over 50, you can enjoy lectures from some top Ivy League educators by attending One Day University held at various colleges. Steven Schragis got the idea for the popular program when he attended a parents weekend at his daughter's college. He saw that the mothers and fathers in the audience were enthralled by the presentations given by the school's best professors.

Schragis finds teachers who are not only fine intellectuals but "brilliant communicators, too." They cover a wide range of topics on any given day. Some of the students may decide to continue their education. Others appreciate the one day jolt of mental stimulation.

All of us need to keep our minds active and engaged and not settle for always doing things in the same way. Try something new today.

An intelligent mind acquires knowledge, and the ear of the wise seeks knowledge. (Proverbs 18:15)

May I stay active and involved in all I do, Spirit of Wisdom.

Not Such Little Matters

It's so easy to get caught up in the everyday aspects of life that we tend to minimize their importance. But just because something seems commonplace may mean that we do not understand the value of each moment of life however insignificant it appears.

One who came to embrace "little things" was St. Thérèse of Lisieux, known as the Little Flower. "Love proves itself by deeds, so how am I to show my love?" she asked. "Great deeds are forbidden me. The only way I can prove my love is by scattering flowers and these flowers are every little sacrifice, every glance and word, and the doing of the least actions for love."

We think ourselves capable of courage, compassion and largeness of spirit. But if we do not practice virtue in small matters, we lack respect for the whole of life God has granted us.

I am setting before you today a blessing...if you obey the commandments of the Lord your God. (Deuteronomy 11:26,27)

Jesus, my Savior, show me how to celebrate every second of the life You grant to me.

Making Mealtime a Message of Love

Move over, prime-time cooking-show hosts! A new superchef is on the horizon: Father Leo Patalinghug.

A seminary professor and the author of *Grace Before Meals: Recipes for Family Life,* Father Leo is now in the production phase of a public-broadcasting network cooking show.

Both the book and the TV show were born of Father Leo's own ministry, in which he encourages families to focus on the communal aspects of cooking and eating, as well as on the importance of gratitude at each meal.

Father Leo also emphasizes the critical role regular family meals can play in a family's happiness and health. "When we eat together as a family, we become more human," he says. He adds that when food is shared together, a community forms.

How often do you break bread with your loved ones? Make shared meals a priority in your home, despite busy schedules.

When He was at the table with them, He took bread, blessed and broke it, and gave it to them. (Luke 24:30)

Give us that daily bread, Father, for which we are eternally grateful.

Raising Awareness, Respecting Life

We humans usually have 23 pairs of chromosomes. Errors result in trisomy, or the presence of an extra chromosome. Birth defects such as Down syndrome can result.

Triathlete Michael Hennessey says of these infants, "It's more important that people become aware of these precious babies." He adds, "God does not make mistakes. See the beauty of God's creation in these amazing little children."

While he and his wife Janelle have six healthy children, friends of theirs have "trisomy kids." So, the triathlete wants to raise awareness of this issue by participating in the most triathlons possible in a single year.

Raising awareness of trisomy and other birth defects is a first step in preventing them, and in treating and caring for these children and their families—from their mothers' wombs to their natural deaths.

The life that is given to us by the Lord is enough for us. (Tobit 5:20)

Whether it's a fetus, a child with a birth defect, or an adult with a terminal illness, help us care for your people tenderly, respectfully, until You call them to Yourself, Lord of life.

Van Gogh and God

Next time you look at a painting by famed artist Vincent Van Gogh, think about "God." The postimpressionist painter was consumed by his Christian faith and by trying to sanctify the secular world.

According to Kathleen Powers Erickson, author of *At Eternity's Gate: The Spiritual Vision of Vincent Van Gogh,* the artist spent his early years reading the book of Isaiah and John Bunyan's *The Pilgrim's Progress.*

Although he sold only one painting while he was alive, Van Gogh felt his life's work was near completion when he painted "Starry Night," his celebration of mystical union with the divine. The sky fills three-quarters of the canvas and is, for Van Gogh, God, the transcendent breath of the Spirit.

The presence of God is all around us—in ourselves, in other people, in earth and sea and sky. Allow that Presence to fill your heart and motivate your actions.

The One who knows all...sends forth the light... called it, and it obeyed Him...called (the stars) and they said, "Here we are!" They shone with gladness for Him who made them. (Baruch 3:32,33,34)

In nature's awesome beauty, I see and praise You, Creator.

Repentance: More than Saying "Sorry"

Sometimes, repentance is confused with being sorry for past wrongs. Repentance is a process by which one thinks deeply of the causes of a past wrong and takes active steps to rectify it. While saying "I'm sorry" can signal regret, it often lacks introspection.

Here's a good example. Every October the Episcopal Church in Philadelphia observes a day of repentance, to confront the past, present and future of the Church's connection with slavery. Some groups even visit Africa and the Caribbean, tracing the route of the slave trade and seeing plantations where slaves were brutalized.

The experience helps participants confront the fact that slavery's legacy involves all Americans.

What in your past needs repentance? An apology helps, but often much more is needed for real redemption.

Two men went up to the temple to pray, one (prayed)... "God, I thank You that I am not like other people"...But the tax collector (said)..."God, be merciful to me, a sinner!" (Luke 18:10,11,13)

Fortify my efforts to face my sins, Merciful Father.

Ahead of the Green Curve

Sharon Rowe knew her then-fledgling business was going to take off. Customers lined up in droves to buy the reusable fabric shopping bags she had designed. In just four hours, Rowe sold 3,000 bags at an Earth Day celebration at $5 apiece.

Today, Eco-Bags Products, Rowe's company in Ossining, New York, has generated millions in sales.

Eco-Bags started in 1989 when Rowe asked a friend to bring her back a string shopping bag from Europe. Rowe liked the idea that the bags were lightweight and easy to use for spur-of-the-moment purchases. Rowe's goal then and now is to clean up the planet "one bag at a time."

One idea can spark change. One person with just one idea can make a huge difference.

Be courageous and valiant. (2 Samuel 13:28)

Help me to be fearless in effecting positive change, Holy Redeemer.

Questions for Mother

Is there something you've always wanted to ask your Mom? Judith Newman, writing in *Real Simple* magazine, suggests questions to help improve your relationship. Try asking:

- Why did you choose to marry my father?
- Do you think it's easier or harder to be a mother today?
- What's one thing, as a mother, you would have done differently?
- How am I like you?
- Is there anything you have always wanted to tell me but haven't?
- Is there anything that you wish had been different between us or that you would still like to change?
- Is there anything you regret not having asked your parents?
- What's the best thing I can do for you right now?

Use the answers to better understand and draw closer to Mom and the rest of your family.

The Lord...confirms a mother's right over her children. (Sirach 3:2)

God, bless families with respectful, intelligent and loving mothers.

On the Road Again

New York City firefighter and triathlete Matthew Long believed he'd never again run the New York City Marathon. He'd been critically injured when a chartered bus pinned him to the pavement while he was biking to work.

His right shoulder, pelvis, both legs, torso and gastrointestinal system had to be extensively repaired. He had skin and muscle grafts.

Yet, in October of 2008, he stood, huffing, puffing and hobbling among the runners preparing for the Marathon. How? Long diligently adhered to his doctors' and surgeons' orders and kept saying to himself and to others, "I will run again."

His gait is uneven, his stride not exactly smooth, the pain constant. However, Long has regained much of his muscle tone and body mass and completed a 3-mile race at 18-minutes a mile.

No one wants to face adversity. But there's no doubt that it can be used to reach new heights of accomplishment.

Though the Lord may give you the bread of adversity and the water of affliction, yet your Teacher will not hide himself any more. (Isaiah 30:20)

When I'm pessimistic, Jesus, gather me up in Your arms.

Two Unique Survivors

Albie had been tightly hogtied at a slaughter-house before he broke free. Animal Care and Control officers caught the malnourished, sickly goat with the infected left leg and sent him to the Woodstock Farm Animal Sanctuary. There, that infected leg had to be amputated just above the knee.

If anyone could care for a 3-½ legged goat it was Jenny Brown, who runs the sanctuary. She lost her own right leg to bone cancer when she was 10. Boogie, a kitten, had accompanied her through girlhood chemo. Then, after producing videos at stockyards in Texas, Brown decided to run the animal refuge.

Her prosthesis enables her to "run a farm... wrestle animals...carry bales of hay." Now, because Albie must do an awkward hop to propel himself, Brown's own prosthetist is crafting an artificial leg for the goat.

Remember to care for and respect all life.

Animals...birds...plants...(and) fish...will declare... (that) in His hand is the life of every living thing and the breath of every human being. (Job 12:7,8,10)

Help us revel in being Your creatures, Creation's Lord.

Tough Times Call for Creativity

The economic downturn has taken its toll on just about every area of life, including education.

Luckily, there are creative individuals working to fill the gap. Episcopal diocesan and parish day camps across the country aim to fill the void as school districts do away with music and art curricula.

In Lexington, North Carolina, children attended a music and art day camp, some for the first time in their lives. During the weeklong camp, participants played piano, guitar or violin, and joined drama and dance classes, all taught by professional musicians and actors.

"It feeds the soul," says the Rev. Bonnie Duckworth, who helped initiate one of the camps. "The connection between arts and the inner spirit is neglected."

Music and art indeed feed the soul, and offer insight into who we are as human beings.

(God) filled them with skill to do every...work done by an artisan or by a designer or by an embroiderer...in fine linen, or by a weaver. (Exodus 35:35)

Enliven our spirits and our lives with all the arts, Spirit of Joy.

Lady Liberty—Remember Her?

Maybe familiarity doesn't breed contempt as much as neglect. Take the Statue of Liberty. It's become such an icon and symbol of America that many New Yorkers who live within easy traveling distance say they have never visited the site.

But considering Lady Liberty's history, she's worth a closer look. Inspired by the colonists' revolutionary heroism, sculptor Frederic August Bartholdi wanted to create an impressive monument to honor them. The 150 foot high sculpture was shipped to the United States from France in 1886 in over 200 immense crates.

All these years later, Lady Liberty is rich with history and symbolism and is not only a national icon but a great work of art.

Value the rights and freedom that the Statue of Liberty represents. Use those same rights and freedom to serve the good of all.

Proclaim liberty throughout the land to all its inhabitants. (Leviticus 25:10)

Protect us and guide us, Author of our liberties.

For What We Take for Granted

The Council of Indian Nations offers a thought-provoking prayer that is well worth considering:

"O Great Spirit, when I have food
Help me to remember the hungry;
When I have work...the jobless;
...a home, those who have no home at all;
When I am without pain...those who suffer;
And remembering,
Help me to destroy my complacency;
Bestir my compassion,
And be concerned enough to help;
By word and deed,
Those who cry out for what we take for granted."

Remember. Give your time, your talents, and if you are able, your treasure, to help those who do not enjoy all that you do.

Oppressing the poor in order to enrich oneself, and giving to the rich, will lead only to loss. (Proverbs 22:16)

God, may my gratitude for all I have, find its expression in thoughtful deeds for others.

For the Children

Karen Gordon, former wife of a Hollywood producer, took her divorce settlement and changed lives. Although she had always been interested in child development, on a research trip to Central American orphanages, Gordon saw children left in their high chairs and others in rooms without toys, taking their boredom out on each other.

Since that trip, Gordon has donated over $1 million to Whole Child International (WCI), a non-profit organization she began to transform these orphanages into nurturing places. Caregivers are being retrained and the environment improved. WCI works with orphanages in El Salvador and Nicaragua; Africa will be next.

"Money doesn't make me happy," she says. "Seeing these children change does."

The future of children is in our hands. We can help those we know and those we don't. Begin by spending time with a needy child.

Jesus said, "Let the little children come to Me, and do not stop them; for it is to such as these that the kingdom of heaven belongs." (Matthew 19:14)

Child Jesus, what child needs my assistance?

Baking Goodness

Greyston Bakery in Yonkers, New York, provides both the brownies for Ben & Jerry's ice cream and fair wages and benefits for their workers.

Founded in 1982, the bakery also sponsors the Greyston Foundation, which supports initiatives for child care, housing, health care, and job and education programs. Toward that end, the bakery has introduced the Do-Goodie Brownie, available at local grocery stores. All profits from brownie sales benefit Foundation projects.

"Most people want to do good in some way but can sometimes be overwhelmed by the enormity of causes," says Julius Walls Jr., president of Greyston Bakery. "The concept of the Do-Goodie is a simple, easy way for consumers to feed their conscience and their love of chocolate."

Every action to serve others—no matter how great or small—helps write our own personal legacy of goodness.

Whoever is faithful in a very little is faithful also in much. (Luke 16:10)

You fill my life with good things, Lord. Help me to share my blessings with others.

Calm Down!

It doesn't take much to get many of us riled up. In fact, given worldwide political unrest, an uncertain economic outlook and other woes, the evening news can feed anyone's anxiety.

What's a worrywart to do? Psychologists suggest a few daily habits to keep us calm despite the turbulence around us.

Move! Such daily exercise as walking can lower the levels of stress hormones in our systems.

Take a deep breath. Stress can cause us to become oxygen deficient, even lightheaded. Deep breathing can also serve to decrease stress-related chemicals in the human body.

Go to sleep. A good night's rest is perhaps one of the best ways to counter stress.

Say thank-you, sincerely and often. Each day, ask yourself, "What new and good thing happened to me today?" Putting some gratitude in your attitude can help calm your inner worrywart.

I will comfort them, and give them gladness for sorrow. (Jeremiah 31:13)

Gracious Father, wrap me in the comforting arms of the Holy Spirit so I may thrive amidst life's challenges.

It's Never Too Late

Until the 1950s or 1960s, bat mitzvahs for Jewish girls coming of age were rare. Even later, they were sometimes not held on Saturday or in a synagogue, nor were the young women allowed to read from the Torah. So recently, a few 90-something women decided to be bas mitzvah!

Ten women at Menorah Park Senior Residence near Cleveland, Ohio, studied for their bat mitzvahs led by Rabbi Howard Kutner. Then one Saturday, each stood to read the prayers in Hebrew and gave a reflection on the Torah passage. Together they sang the hymns. Finally, they had officially become religious adults, responsible for observing the Commandments, able to lead religious services, to form binding contracts, and to count in a minyan (the ten adults needed for religious services).

Whatever your age, express your spiritual life.

The righteous flourish like the palm tree... planted in the house of the Lord; they flourish in the courts of our God. In old age they still produce fruit. (Psalm 92:12,13,14)

Encourage us to celebrate our spirituality at every age, Ancient of Days.

Welcome to the Church of Punk

It's an odd mixture: teens between 15 and 19, punk-rock music and a church. Yet, the blend has resulted in a much-needed site for gathering, dancing and fellowship for young people in a neighborhood that doesn't offer them many other options.

Each month, the First Lutheran Church of Throggs Neck, New York, offers its basement to The Bronx Underground, a local concert promoter, to host concerts by up-and-coming punk bands.

The event draws large crowds of eager fans, most dressed in black lipstick, colorfully dyed hair, thick eyeliner and large, chunky metal adornments.

When neighbors expressed concern about the noise, a community association worked with everyone on a compromise. The teens quelled unreasonable noise; neighbors learned to be more tolerant.

Wholesome community gathering places can help make a neighborhood a better place for teens and adults.

There is a season, and a time for every matter under heaven...a time to laugh...and a time to dance. (Ecclesiastes 3:1,4)

Improve intergenerational respect and communication, Jesus.

A Horse Tale

What happens to a racehorse when it's stopped running? Does it roam forever through grassy meadows? Does it enjoy a lifetime of fresh hay and apples? Not quite. Many thoroughbreds earn a one-way ticket to the slaughterhouse. LumberJack Farm seeks to prevent this unfortunate end.

Located in New Jersey, LumberJack Farm is a rehabilitation facility for retired and injured racehorses. The farm operates under ReRun, a non-profit organization which gives horses a second chance at life. Laurie Condurso-Lane, president of ReRun, laments the horses' treatment, saying, "'They are young. So why not find them new jobs?'"

Just because a racehorse has finished its career on the track does not mean life is over. Be kind to our animal friends.

**You shall rise before the aged, and defer to the old; and you shall fear your God.
(Leviticus 19:32)**

Help us, God, to value not only the wisdom and skills, but especially the lives of the aged, human and animal alike.

Making Memories

Stay-at-home mom Linda Cook missed the social interaction she had when she worked outside her home. So, by the time her two sons were pre-schoolers, she decided it was time to find a volunteer opportunity.

Her fondness for seniors led her to a local assisted-living facility that sought volunteers to interact with elderly residents. Best of all, the staff welcomed Cook's sons, who could also volunteer by playing cards and chatting with residents. Cook was thrilled.

That was 15 years ago. Cook's enthusiasm and commitment to her volunteer work eventually led to a paid position. What Cook holds most dear about the whole experience is the wisdom that the aging residents have imparted to her. Said one woman, "When you're older, memories are all you have. So make them good ones!"

Live each day so as to weave a rich tapestry of memories that will last a lifetime.

My days are swifter than a weaver's shuttle. (Job 7:6)

Remind me, Father, that You are beside me at the weaver's bench, helping me weave each day's memories.

Breathing Easier

Did you know that indoor air quality can affect your health? Here are some tips to help:

Rather than wheezing and sneezing and getting a headache, open the windows. Avoid air fresheners.

Also avoid cleaning sprays and harsh cleaning chemicals, but do clean and dust frequently. Don't wear street shoes indoors.

Keep humidity low. Vent the laundry and bathrooms. Watch for dampness and leaks in the cellar; use a dehumidifier.

Use organic wool, cotton, coir or jute rugs that have not been treated with chemicals or glues. Steam clean only.

Keep electronics in one room: toner cartridges contain nickel and mercury; computers, have toxic gases, metals, acids and plastics.

Your home is your castle. Keep it as clean and healthful as you can.

He left Nazareth and made His home in Capernaum by the sea, in the territory of Zebulun and Naphtali. (Matthew 4:13)

Abide with us, Jesus.

The $5 Song That Made Lincoln Cry

During America's Civil War, soldiers on both sides often sang, *John Brown's Body*, the tale of abolitionist John Brown. The North viewed him as a martyr; the South celebrated his execution.

Then Julia Ward Howe, a Boston poet and activist, wrote the moving *Battle Hymn of the Republic* which became the anthem of the Union. Howe's song, which moved President Abraham Lincoln to tears, was first published as a poem in *Atlantic Monthly* in February 1862. She was paid five dollars for it.

Although Howe continued her writings about causes near and dear to her heart, none had the impact of the *Battle Hymn of the Republic*. It became a truly national song, sung by American troops in the Spanish American War and World Wars I and II.

All you do and say and—even sing—should reflect the values that affirm and acknowledge God's own special spark within you and others.

They shall beat their swords into plowshares, and their spears into pruning hooks; nation shall not lift up sword against nation, neither shall they learn war any more. (Micah 4:3)

May my words and actions celebrate the spark of Your peace-filled life within me, Creator.

Feeding Your Family Takes More than Food

There's more to nourishing a family than the food they need to stay alive and healthy. Families need spiritual and emotional sustenance to stay close, according to experts. So, to help keep a family together, experts suggest the following tips:

- Make everyday moments, say carpooling and grocery shopping, a time of connection, rather than a mundane task.

- Speak respectfully, even when upset. Psychologists agree that the damage caused by sarcastic jibes and putdowns lasts long beyond one's recollection of a disagreement.

- Reach out and touch one another with nonverbal but necessary and powerful messages of love. A hug can go a long way in communicating appreciation and love.

- Create shared experiences to cement lasting memories. Says one professor, "Close families build history."

Seek out every opportunity to sweeten and strengthen your family's bond.

Let love be genuine. (Roman 12:9)

I am blessed to be a member of Your family, Heavenly Father!

A Present that Doesn't Match Her Past

Do you assume that a highly successful person must have come from privileged beginnings? Wealth and privilege can ease one's path, but it's certainly not the rule.

Helene Gayle, chief executive officer of CARE USA, a leading humanitarian organization fighting global poverty, is one person who defied the odds to become a success. Born to modest beginnings in Buffalo, New York, Gayle was hit by a car when she was 12 years old. Shortly thereafter, her parents divorced. Her mother's chronic mental illness took a toll on Gayle and her siblings, and, as she puts it, "Our lives became less stable."

Gayle sees her childhood injury as a lesson in self-reliance; her mother's illness as an introduction to the world of medicine. She completed medical school and earned a Master's degree in public health. She says this was the result of her family's "focus on helping the community.".

How can you transform a problem into an asset?

We beseech You, give us success! (Psalm 118:25)

Help me trust the wisdom of Your ways, Holy Spirit.

Too Much Stuff

When Dustin Allen was single, he was pretty much able to buy whatever he wanted. "I would fixate on something and go after it like it was a quest," says Allen.

Then he met Christy, a single mom with two kids. "We fell in love, got married, added to our family and our debt," he says. There were always things they felt they needed and their debt kept mounting. "Christy and I couldn't get through one trip to the grocery store without spending more than we had," Allen admits.

Feeling as though he had lost control, Allen prayed, "I have to get out of this mess, Lord. Please help me." The family whittled down its debt, held garage sales, sold unnecessary possessions. The result? Debt slashed by $36,000 and money in an emergency fund, too.

Appreciate how wealthy we are; how little we need for a satisfying, enriching life.

One's life does not consist in the abundance of possessions. (Luke 12:15)

Teach me prudence and restraint in my spending, Lord Jesus.

From Stillness to Serenity

Fran Hart was devastated when she re-injured her spinal column after difficult and painful neck surgery. Anytime she sat, stood up or merely lifted her head, spinal fluid would leak from her brain, triggering extreme nausea and painful headaches. Her doctor ordered bed rest.

Hart was speechless. Until then, her life had been defined by a demanding work and family schedule. She couldn't imagine lying in bed indefinitely. Yet, after a few weeks, the silence, peace and relaxation took over. Meditating, Hart realized, "I knew God was God, and He was telling me, 'Be still,'" she says. After six weeks of rest, she had healed, and, as she says, "Nothing had collapsed" in her absence.

Ultimately, Hart's life changed. "I don't confuse being busy with being faithful, anymore," she says.

There is wisdom to be found in stillness. Take even three minutes a day to simply be.

Keep silence and hear. (Deuteronomy 27:9)

Help quiet the restlessness in my spirit, Prince of Peace.

Pictures from Stones

With a pair of pliers and boundless patience, Manny Vega transforms thousands of stone and glass tesserae (usually cube shaped tiles) into glimmering mosaic portraits of poets, drummers, mothers and sons and daughters.

This mosaicist grew up in New York City where he saw his first mosaic of tropical fish that still adorns an Art Deco building not far from Yankee Stadium.

Studying art in high school and then continuing with art school, Vega experimented with painting, but was drawn to mosaics. "Paint fades," he said.

"Everybody wants instant art," Vega explained. "This is old school. A good design, some good materials, and shut up and do the work. There is no shortcut."

No matter the task, our hard work, backed by a loving heart and God's splendid design can make anything possible.

Commit your work to the Lord. (Proverbs 16:3)

May the work of my hands give You praise, Creator.

Why Can't I Be the Mayor?

Nearly 35 per cent of the indigenous women of Mexico are illiterate. They are both poor and marginalized. Why? Tradition!

Zapoteca Eufrosina Cruz is appalled by this. She left her hometown rather than be married off at 13. And she was self supporting while becoming an accountant and then the coordinator of academic programs in Oaxaca's technical high schools.

When Cruz tried to run for mayor of Quiegolani she was denied because she was a woman. That's when she began *Quiego,* which holds workshops to help women understand that not all traditions are good, and to raise women's awareness of their political rights.

Because she had received death threats, Eufrosina Cruz left her high school position rather than "endanger my bosses, who supported me."

Encourage boys and girls, men and women to seek justice and exercise equal rights.

I commend to you our sister Phoebe, a deacon of the church...Prisca...Mary...and Junia...prominent among the apostles. (Romans 16:1,3,6,7)

God, help women and men to respect and value one another as individuals.

Do You Hear Me, God?

Do we ever consider God's answer when we pray? Do we really listen? Often we are so focused on venting or asking for things that we never hear His response.

When Ada Duncan became involved with her son's study for first Communion, she learned that "Prayer is talking and listening to God." But, Duncan asked herself, "how does one listen to God?"

She learned to hear God's voice in the answer to a prayer of petition; in a solution to a problem; in what others said to her; in a touch. Duncan adds, "my prayers are no longer memorized words or a monologue with a distant Being. They have become a conversation with a dear Friend, with whom I share even the most mundane and insignificant things...I always know He has heard me because when I listen, I can hear His voice."

Enjoy a conversation with God!

(There was) a sound of sheer silence. When Elijah heard it, he wrapped his face in his mantle. (1 Kings 19:12-13)

Let's have a conversation, Eternal Word, ever near me.

Being Bigger than Our Troubles

Even if you are generally upbeat and walk on the sunny side of street, you cannot ignore the surprises, sometimes painful ones, life has in store for each one of us.

Nonetheless, you can always make your own choices about how to handle the painful problems that come your way.

Advice columnist Ann Landers put it this way, "If I were asked to give what I consider the single most useful bit of advice for all humanity, it would be this: Expect trouble as an inevitable part of life and when it comes, hold your head high, look it squarely in the eye and say, 'I will be bigger than you. You cannot defeat me.'"

If you keep hope in your heart, trust God's strength and guidance and do the very best you can everyday, no matter what others may think, your spirit will never be conquered.

Blessed be the Lord, who daily bears us up. (Psalm 68:19)

Gracious Lord, in Your courage and compassion, let me find the power to live my life with enthusiasm and gladness.

Century-Old Shop Comes to an End

Thomas De Lorenzo was part of the third generation of his family to own and operate a metalwork shop. Founded in 1907, the shop was located in Manhattan's SoHo district, south of Houston Street.

Back in 1907, the area was a gritty, industrial district with rough-and-tumble enterprises. It remained so until the 1970s, when SoHo's lower commercial rents began attracting struggling artists, sculptors and designers.

The De Lorenzos had new clients who often came in with only a sketch and an idea. In time, however, that changed. Rising rents drove away most shops and artists. Recently, the De Lorenzo family business was bought out by a condominium developer. A longtime associate says, "They helped many, many artists. This place is really the last of its kind."

Our impact on others can outlast us. How do you want to be remembered by those you love?

In the memory of virtue is immortality...when it is present, people imitate it, and they long for it when it has gone. (Wisdom of Solomon 4:1,2)

Steer me toward a life of ethical choices, Father God.

The Ten (Political) Commandments

With the Ten Commandments in mind, here are some thoughts on politics and citizenship:

1. Do not put all your hopes in a political or economic theory or party line.
2. Do not worship political figures or images.
3. God does not belong to your political party nor does God endorse your political opinion.
4. Do not use God to support your political theories.
5. Respect the political views of other family members.
6 Disagree but don't be cruel or disrespectful.
7. Do not inject politics into every conversation.
8. Be honest when you vote; consider being a poll worker.
9. Defend the truth even if that makes you unpopular.
10. Accept ballot results without gloating or moaning.

Use your God-given intellect and free will for the peace-filled common good.

I turned my mind to know and...to seek wisdom and the sum of things. (Ecclesiastes 7:25)

Help me be an insightful citizen and voter, Holy Spirit.

"Coming, Lord"

There's a saint you may not have heard of named Alphonsus Rodriguez. If you haven't, he wouldn't mind; he was a very humble man.

He lived in 17th century Spain. While in his thirties, his business failed and his wife and children died. He wanted to become a priest, but was prevented by poor health and minimal education. Eventually, he became a Jesuit lay brother, serving as the doorkeeper at the order's college in Majorca for over forty years.

This gentle man became a sought-after spiritual advisor to students, staff and local townspeople. Brother Alphonsus had a singular way of doing his job and living his life. He imagined that everyone who came to the door was Jesus. So, as he opened the door, he smiled and said to himself, "I'm coming, Lord!"

How wonderful if we could greet others in the same way: "I'm coming, Lord!"

**Greet every saint in Christ Jesus.
(Philippians 4:21)**

Jesus, please let me see Your beautiful face in every person I meet.

In Times of Grief

Do you feel awkward around someone who is bereaved? Do you want to say something comforting but don't know what?

Robbie Miller Kaplan wrote a book for just such a situation. It's called *How to Say It When You Don't Know What to Say*. Having suffered the death of two infant children, she came to realize that many people want to help but don't know how. She offers these suggestions:

- Accept that you are an integral part of the grieving process. Mourners must have a strong support network to cope with the death of a loved one.
- Allow the bereaved to talk about the deceased as often or for as long as they would like.
- Share your special memories of the deceased.
- Be there for the duration.

Never let your own fears keep you from reaching out in compassion to someone suffering the loss of a loved one.

Lazarus had already been in the tomb four days. ...Many...had come to Martha and Mary to console them about their brother. (John 11:17,19)

Merciful Father, guide my efforts to console my grieving brothers and sisters.

As You Did It to One of the Least...

Founded by Daughter of Charity Sister Bernadette Szymczak, St. John's Bread and Life Center has become Brooklyn's largest soup kitchen.

Bread and Life is not traditional. Instead, it offers clients computers on which they can choose the food they want from the food pyramid. Clients receive something similar to a credit card, a PIN number, and credits that are renewed every month.

While they wait for the food they requested, clients sit in a sky-lighted lounge area with wood-and-leather benches and a library. These changes provide a healthier and more decent experience for the needy.

What can you do to help those in need? Remember, every human being regardless of any labels we may put on them, deserves respect, comfort, proper care, and health-sustaining nutrition.

I was hungry and you gave Me food...thirsty and you gave Me...drink...a stranger and you welcomed Me...naked and you gave Me clothing. (Matthew 25:34,35,36)

Remind us of the common humanity which we share with the poor, the sick and the homeless, Creator of all.

Be a Book Booster!

Writer Angela Shelf wasn't aware of her impact on children. She was just showing her own passion for reading as she visited schools and shared stories from her many children's books.

Teachers began telling her that after seeing her presentation students who didn't like to read wanted to learn.

Shelf thought, "Why not help kids before they're struggling and starting to hate reading?" With the help of her husband and family, Book Boosters was created. Before long, 23 Austin, Texas, elementary schools offered tutoring by the after-school program. Also, kids receive their own books from Book Boosters.

Lesson learned? "If you share your passions, you can make a world of difference for somebody," says Shelf

Change the world for the better today for a child or an adult.

Always seek to do good to one another and to all. (1 Thessalonians 5:15)

Inspire our efforts to support and encourage teachers, God.

Keeping the Doctor Away

Would you like to stay healthy during the cold and flu season? Then show compassion every-day! Research shows that altruism can positively affect your well-being.

"It's good to be good, and science proves it," says researcher Stephen Post of Case Western Reserve University School of Medicine. Try these ideas:

- Volunteer at a literacy program, soup kitchen or animal shelter.
- Mentor a child or visit nursing home residents.
- See how you can help those in recovery. Volunteer at a hotline.
- Join or begin a support group for people coping with a chronic serious illness if you yourself are dealing with a such a problem.
- Invite a friend to join your volunteering efforts

Just remember, the compassion you show to others is the compassion you show to your self.

Clothe yourselves with compassion. (Colossians 3:12)

Inspire me to imitate Your compassion, Jesus.

A New Greed

Today, when it seems as though computers and cell phones are revamped every other month, people want *new*. Ah, but the question is: do they really *need* new?

According to Alice Camille, co-author of *The Forgiveness Book,* it's not material worth we should be concerned about, but our true selves.

How can we change ourselves, rather than our surroundings? Camille believes that our constant desire for more derives from original sin. She adds that the only way to become a new person is to "have faith in the God of the New and allow that God to plant a new heart and new spirit within you."

Improving ourselves is far from easy, but it can be accomplished by God's grace and with determination and patience. Focus on being the best you can be instead of worrying about what's new.

Get yourselves a new heart and a new spirit! (Ezekiel 18:31)

Teach us to value a heart and spirit attentive to Your eternal values and verities, God of the Covenant.

Optimistically Speaking

It probably won't surprise you that the word pessimism comes from the Latin for worst; optimism from the word for best. What does it mean to live optimistically?

In *Creed for Optimists,* Christian Larsen wrote: "Be so strong that nothing can disturb you peace of mind. Talk health, happiness and prosperity to every person you meet. Make all your friends feel there is something in them. Look at the sunny side of everything. Think only of the best, work only for the best, and expect only the best.

"Be as enthusiastic about the success of others as you are about your own. Forget the mistakes of the past and press on to the greater achievements of the future. Give everyone a smile. Spend so much time improving yourself that you have no time left to criticize others. Be too big for worry and too noble for anger."

Be gentle with yourself, yet strive to do your best.

A joyful heart is life itself. (Sirach 30:22)

Spirit of Joy, nurture my heart and soul. Add zest to my desire to seek Your will in all I am and all I do.

A New Beginning

The Rockefeller Foundation awarded a Jane Jacobs Medal to Alexie Torres-Fleming, executive director of the Youth Ministries for Peace and Justice, for her efforts at urban renewal in the Soundview/Bruckner area of the South Bronx. Torres-Fleming and her group transformed a former crack house into a desirable rental in a much improved neighborhood.

Torres-Fleming also directed youth outreach and arts programs, attracted economic development and supervised environmental and fiscal education programs. She promoted ecological initiatives on the Bronx River where a concrete plant was abandoned. A 10-acre park will provide locals with a dock, beach, reading area, gardens and, eventually, an amphitheater.

With her faith, prayers, and determination, one woman helped transform her neighborhood. How can you improve yours?

She was devoted to good works. (Acts 9:36)

Bless us with the determination and skills to make our neighborhoods better, Lord.

Spreading Shalom

The "Grand Dragon of the White Knights of the Ku Klux Klan," Larry Trapp, sent hate messages to Rabbi Michael Weisser. Trapp later admitted he "went out of my way to instill fear."

Instead, Rabbi Weisser left his own messages about love and acceptance like, "Larry, there's a lot of love out there. Don't you want some?' and "Larry, why do you love the Nazis? They'd have killed you first because you're disabled (both legs had been amputated because of diabetes and he was almost blind)."

Eventually Trapp phoned saying, "I want to get out of what I'm doing and I don't know how." The rabbi and his wife visited Trapp. Then, as he became sicker, they took him into their home. Trapp renounced the Klan, apologized, and converted to Judaism. He died less than a year after he had met Rabbi Weisser. The Rabbi adds, "an act of kindness can make a change."

Make changes. Be kind.

Show kindness and mercy to one another. (Zechariah 7:9)

Holy Spirit, give us the courage to be gracious in the face of rudeness; kind in the face of hatred and bigotry; just in the face of injustice.

Going Green Adds Green to Your Wallet

"Going green" signals a greater awareness of our Earth and a heightened mindfulness of caring for the only home we've got.

But did you know that what's good for the planet is often good for your purse, too? Diane MacEachern, an expert on environmentalism, makes these cost-efficient, planet-friendly tips:

- Drink tap water not bottled, and reduce plastic consumption.
- Ditch paper towels, and use cloth instead. You'll save a tree.
- Eat less meat. You'll save cash and lessen pollution from meat production.
- When mowing your lawn, leave grass clippings on the ground; you'll avoid using plastic bags while fertilizing your yard.
- Don't trash it. Reuse it. For instance, recycle old tablecloths into napkins or dust cloths.

Creativity can keep your planet and your wallet green!

It is required of stewards that they be found trustworthy. (1 Corinthians 4:2)

Protect our blessed earth, Great Creator who formed it.

Send a Soldier a Guitar

When Steve Baker returned home to Minnesota after four years in Vietnam, he felt stunned and directionless. "I became angry, a drinker, stumbling from job to job," he recalls.

But he still had his music, a part of his life since childhood. Baker started playing guitar again. Performing gave him something to look forward to, helped him quit drinking, and eventually provided enough money for Baker to open his own music store.

Knowing the healing power of music, he sent a guitar to his stepson who was serving in Iraq. Other soldiers soon started requesting instruments, telling how music eased the stress of war.

To date, Baker has sent more than 550 guitars to U.S. troops; some bought with money raised through community fundraisers, and others donated.

What heals our pain may soothe another's suffering too.

David took the lyre and played it...and Saul would...feel better. (1 Samuel 16:23)

Merciful Savior, inspire us to use music to soothe and heal broken minds and spirits.

The Luck of the Duck

Laura Backman lives in Portsmouth, Rhode Island, with her pet duck, Lemon. Lemon is no ordinary duck—she was born disabled. Her neurological disability affects her balance and so she waddles with the assistance of a device made from PVC pipes with four coasters as wheels.

Despite her physical limitations, Lemon has become a source of comfort to others. Backman has taken her to a camp for physically-handicapped children called Confidence is Cool. The experience spurred Backman to continue Lemon's work as a therapy duck. Backman chronicles her and Lemon's adventures on the website LemontheDuck.com.

Respect and assist individuals who suffer from physical and mental challenges. They might be restricted in body or mind, but not in spirit, with your encouragement and respect.

You shall not revile the deaf or put a stumbling block before the blind; you shall fear your God; I am the Lord. (Leviticus 19:14)

God, help us be gentle, patient and respectful with one another, especially with persons with disabilities.

For a Better Life

Consider these thoughts for a better, happier life:

- Smile and laugh more.
- Remember that life is good if not always fair.
- Agree to disagree instead of trying to win every argument.
- Make peace with your past lest it spoil your present.
- Forgive everyone for everything.
- Keep in touch with your family and friends.
- No matter how you feel, get up, dress up and show up.
- Remove the clutter from your environment.
- Play games, read books, enjoy music.

Life is your school. You are the pupil. Your curriculum includes problems. Tackle them in a positive way. Don't waste energy or time on what you can not control. Do all you can with God's help to make your life the best life possible.

The days of our life are seventy years, or perhaps eighty, if we are strong...They are soon gone, and we fly away. (Psalm 90:10)

Guide our efforts to live the best life we can, Abba.

Loved—One by One

With almost seven billion people on this planet of ours, we can sometimes forget just how truly one-of-a-kind we are.

God created each of us to be unique; He loves us as individuals. Cardinal John Henry Newman, the 19th century writer, Anglican priest and then Catholic cardinal, said this about God's overwhelmingly personal love:

"God beholds you. He calls you by name. He sees you and understands you as He made you. He knows what is in you, all your peculiar feelings and thoughts, your dispositions and likings, your strength and your weakness.

"He encompasses you round and bears you in His arms. He notes your very countenance, whether smiling or in tears. He looks tenderly upon you. He hears your voice, the beating of your heart and your very breathing. You do not love yourself better than He loves you."

God loves you—uniquely, distinctly, specially. And He always will.

Know the Lord. (Hosea 2:20)

Thank You, Spirit of Love, for Yourself and for myself.

It's Just Water, Right?

Turning on the tap and running the water is something we do so often, most of us do not give it a second thought. But what if you turned on the faucet and nothing came out for weeks or months?

In Darfur, Sudan, getting potable water has always been a challenge due to civil unrest, droughts, distance and a faulty infrastructure.

Recently, though, hope has emerged in the form of a large steel water tank. Catholic Relief Services (CRS), in partnership with UNICEF and the Sudanese government, has set up a water system in West Darfur that transports drinkable water considerable distances. It reaches small villages filled with refugees from political unrest and violence. Says one refugee, "It is good to have the tap here. It saves time for making food."

Funny how something many take for granted could be seen as a life-changing gift. Take stock of the conveniences you enjoy daily, remembering that others would consider them luxuries.

In the beginning...a wind from God swept over the face of the waters. (Genesis 1:2)

Help me appreciate Your gift of life-sustaining water, Creator.

A Child's Helping Hand

How old do you have to be to aid those less fortunate than you are?

John Butsch of Mason, Ohio, was not yet six when he asked his mom, "Do you know what I'd like for my birthday? I want to help people."

His mother Marianne Butsch, writing in *Guideposts*, says that she was touched. She organized a "Bowl for Bucks" party for John and twenty of his friends. Guests contributed money instead of toys or other gifts and the Butsch family added $5 for each spare or strike. That raised $470 which they sent to Cincinnati's City Gospel Mission along with a picture of the party-goers.

In turn the mission invited John to meet the staff and the residents he had helped in such a thoughtful way.

What opportunity will you use today to reach out to those in need?

**Open your hand to the poor.
(Deuteronomy 15:11)**

Merciful Redeemer, inspire me in using my imagination to help my brothers and sisters who need assistance.

Enjoy the Holidays!

Are you enjoying the start of the holiday season? You can, if you focus on what really matters.

- Regardless of your faith tradition, nurture it.
- Take time for yourself. Do not rush through the holidays. Cultivate quiet time.
- Be temperate with food, drink and treats as well as parties and activities.
- Take what comes. Accept your imperfect family and friends. Do not expect perfect presents.
- Enjoy what you can and ignore the rest. Do not try to control others. Respect your own feelings.
- Know your finances, avoid debt and don't try to impress anyone.

Try these tips and you will enjoy the whole season!

Rejoice and exult with all your heart. (Zephaniah 3:14)

Fill me with Your own joy, God.

Help for Home Owners

Terry Williams and members of the JustFaith organization in Cheyenne, Wyoming, developed the Wyoming Family Home Ownership Project (WYFHOP), a project that gives low-income families the opportunity to grow financially while creating lasting relationships.

Many in the area are struggling. Williams asks, "What can we do that would move them toward true independence and self-sufficiency?" With the help of WYFHOP, participants receive financial literacy training, meet with leadership families, and establish a family home savings account. In addition, for each family, every dollar saved up to the first $2000 will be matched by the Wyoming Women's Business Center.

This project will give families the chance to "achieve the American dream, having a home, living in the community and being successful," says Williams.

With support everyone has a chance for a positive future.

Human success is in the hand of the Lord. (Sirach 10:5)

Remind us to work with You, Lord, to support those struggling to be successful.

Touch a Life, Change a Life

After the death of his 10-year-old daughter, Howard Weinstein lost his job and his zest for life. A job offer in Africa gave him a fresh start while helping others.

Weinstein traveled to Otse, Botswana, where he developed an inexpensive hearing aid powered by rechargeable solar batteries called SolarAid. He also developed a charger that can plug into a wall outlet or use its own built-in solar panel.

Out of 250 million hearing impaired people around the world, two-thirds live in developing nations. Now, people in 30 countries are using Weinstein's hearing aids, chargers and batteries.

"Poor people in Africa, Latin America and Asia wear a hearing device until it runs down and then put it in the drawer or sell it," he says. Weinstein adds that by coming up with a solution, "you could touch millions of lives."

How can you touch just one life today?

**Always seek to do good to one another.
(1 Thessalonians 5:15)**

Inspire many to address insuperable problems at home and abroad with their skills and talents, Jesus.

Gobble Gobble...Squabble Squabble

In the words of a well known hymn, "we gather together to ask the Lord's blessing" every Thanksgiving at the home of the family member with the biggest dining table.

Suddenly, you may find people fighting family feuds of the past! Peace, though, is possible, especially if you plan now.

Don't caricature, make presumptions or label. Lay aside contempt, resentment, impatience and political correctness. Work to judge neither personalities nor habits lest you be judged.

Look for proffered olive branches. Don't expect others to know or remember what offended you—especially if it happened months or even years ago.

Ask what's bothering someone. Don't assume you know what's causing friction. The answer might surprise you.

Then in peace we can continue that hymn: "Beside us to guide us, our God with us joining, ordaining, maintaining, His kingdom divine."

Give thanks to the God of gods for His steadfast love endures forever...who alone does great wonders. (Psalm 136:2,4)

Help us love all the members of our family, Jesus, Son of Joseph and Mary, Son of God.

To Her, Hemlock is Hardly a Pariah

Californian Wendy Johnson loves most all of Earth's living creatures, particularly hemlock. In fact, so great is her reverence for leafy living things, that even the poisonous hemlock plant holds a special place in both Johnson's heart and garden.

Johnson, a Zen gardener who enjoys her garden for meditation and solitude, believes that without the presence of this perennial, her garden would be "boring." Johnson instead welcomes the innocent-looking but dangerous hemlock, which she allows to flourish for its ability to draw rich minerals from the soil for compost. "It gives the garden its punch," she says, "snapping me back to my senses."

One person's poison truly is another's pleasure. Learn to respect others' opinions and values. You will find your life enriched.

Pay...respect to whom respect is due...love one another; for the one who loves another has fulfilled the law. (Romans 13:7,8)

Help us be genuinely and deeply respectful, merciful, patient and kind to one another, Merciful Savior.

A Very Cooperative Food Co-op

The Oklahoma Food Cooperative is, well, cooperative. A cross between a farmers' market and a grocery store, this online-only food mart connects urban Oklahomans with their state's farmers and fresh produce across cyberspace.

While its virtual nature makes the Cooperative unusual, its holistic approach makes it even more so. It's the result of a grassroots network uniting Oklahomans interested in supporting local farmers, and driven by a desire to make more healthful food choices overall. Volunteers of all ages, even children, help support the effort, making the venture truly an exercise in service and cooperation.

The Co-op's Founder, Bob Waldrop, quotes Dorothy Day as saying, "said she worked toward a world where it would be easier for people to behave decently."

Encourage people to behave decently: start with your good example.

Who is a rock besides our God? — the God who girded me with strength, and made my way safe. (Psalm 18:31-32)

Cradle us in Your community, Messiah.

Combating Stress

Stress can be an underlying cause of weight gain. When you're anxious, the release of adrenaline and cortisol causes an insatiable craving for junk food. You gain weight. Nancy Kalish, writing in *Prevention*, offers several suggestions:

- Exercise. Moving your muscles is an effective, instant stress reliever.
- Eat slowly. Don't gobble, enjoy and taste your food.
- Regulate. Three healthy meals and two snacks will satisfy your hunger and limit weight gain.
- Yield a little when you want something that shouldn't be eaten in excess.
- Drink decaf coffee. Caffeine worsens stress.
- Eat a healthy breakfast. Fruit and whole grains lower stress and provide essential vitamins.
- Sleep more than six-and-a-half hours every night.

Take this advice into account and live healthily.

Health and fitness are better than any gold, and a robust body than countless riches. (Sirach 30:15)

Creator, inspire my efforts to gently guide myself into healthier choices in the way I live, in food and in drink.

A Football Game and a Decision

In 1958, racial segregation still shadowed American life. So when the football team at the University of Buffalo (now the State University of New York at Buffalo) was invited to a bowl game in Florida, the players learned that sports is not just fun and games.

The owners of the stadium where the game was to be played refused to let blacks and whites play together. The Bulls were told to take the field without their two black players. The coach and administration left the choice to the players. They never took a vote. The team walked out.

Fifty years later, one of those men said, "If we had given in, gone to the game, we would never have had the camaraderie we have now. We would have always felt we let our buddies down."

Most of those men stayed close over the years. They never let their buddies down—or themselves.

God created humankind...in the likeness of God. Male and female He created them, and He blessed them and named them "Humankind." (Genesis 5:1-2)

Some decisions are harder than others, Holy Spirit. Guide me in always choosing what is good and right.

Thoughts from the Oneida Nation

Among the most popular floats in Macy's 2008 Thanksgiving Day Parade was one sponsored by the Oneida Indian Nation called "The True Spirit of Thanksgiving." Here are excerpts from the Oneidas thought-provoking "thank-you" that appeared in *The New York Times:*

"The gifts from the Creator are precious and are to be shared with everyone. Everything in the natural world is intertwined, and...acting from the Creator's instructions, does its part to keep this world of ours in balance.

"Peace is considered one of the greatest gifts of the Creator. ...The constant watch and protection of Peace (is what) all men should be constantly engaged in.

"...Our job is to tend to all the Creator has given us so they may still be enjoyed seven generations from now, by the faces yet unborn."

Sharing, balance, peace. Work toward these in your personal, family and community life. You and your world will be the better for it.

On the seventh day God finished the work that He had done, and He rested. (Genesis 2:2)

God of loveliness, inspire us to work for balance and harmony.

Shalom/Salaam

Peace. In Hebrew *shalom*. In Arabic *salaam*. The absence of armed conflict with genuine peace among the nations? Yes. But also, genuine peace, individual completeness; welfare; well-being; safety. Wouldn't it be a God-send if this peace covered our Earth?

With this in mind here are excerpts from a prayer for peace from the Victorious Missionaries:

"Lord of peace...Your designs are for peace, not affliction. ...Reunite people of all races and descent in a single family. Hear the...plea of all humanity for peace. ...Stop the desire for retaliation and revenge. Suggest...new solutions, generous and honorable gestures, time for patient waiting. Amen."

Pray for peace. Live peace. Make peace. Be peace. *Shalom aleichem...Assalamu alaikum* — Peace and well-being be upon you!

Blessed are the peacemakers, for they will be called children of God. (Matthew 5:9)

Lord of peace, teach us to be peace for our selves, our family, neighbors and coworkers; for the world.

Talking Trash

In Lahore, Pakistan, a handful of young adults have banded together to form Responsible Citizens. This group is dedicated to the betterment of their community by cleaning up the garbage littering their streets.

Though many disagree with the friends' efforts, saying change is impossible in a country where political and economic issues have widened the class gap, the group is unwavering. Members of Responsible Citizens say that by gathering trash, recruiting more workers, and alerting inhabitants as to proper trash disposal, everyone will become more organized and conditions will improve.

Murtaza Khwaja, one of the Responsible Citizens, says, "We have to lead by example. To change it from inside."

Lead by example. Get involved. What can you do for your neighborhood?

Let us set an example. (Judith 8:24)

Give me the perseverance necessary to lead by example, Gracious God.

Advent and Christmas for Two

Think Advent and Christmas celebrations are mainly for children? Not according to Renae Bottom in *Today's Christian Woman*. Here are her suggestions for couples at holiday time:

- During Advent make time at least weekly to light candles and read to each other from seasonal poems, stories or Scripture
- Microwave popcorn. Watch holiday movies. *A Christmas Story, It's a Wonderful Life, The Nativity,* are examples.
- Volunteer together.
- Choose a special entrée or dessert you can prepare together for a special holiday meal for two
- Make an special "Merry Christmas" toast to each other.

Advent and Christmas are celebrations of God's love made flesh. What better time to celebrate your love for each other?

In this is love, not that we loved God but that He loved us and sent His Son to be the atoning sacrifice for our sins. (1 John 4:10)

Refresh and revitalize couples' love for each other, loving Father.

An Actresses' Best Role

To most people, Marcia Gay Harden is a talented Oscar winning actress. But to a little girl dying of cancer, she was really Snow White.

Like many before her, when she started out Harden had to pay her dues as a struggling young actor waiting on tables and rushing to open casting calls. But she knew she was meant to act. "There was a quality about acting that made me feel in touch with something big and mysterious and meaningful." The right role could make her feel "that God was using me for something good".

As a young actress, Harden told the Make-A-Wish Foundation she would play Snow White to grant a dying 7-year-old's request. But then the date conflicted with an important casting call. Ultimately she chose what she now views as her best role ever to help a little girl who died a week later.

We all have choices to make. What will you choose today?

Am I not allowed to do what I choose? (Matthew 20:15)

Guide and inspire our decision making, Jesus.

Expectations for All

John Wooden, the legendary UCLA basketball coach, had certain expectations for his players. They make sense for all of us to consider:

- Be a gentleman (or gentlewoman) at all times.
- Never criticize, nag or razz others.
- Be a team player as much as possible.
- Never be selfish, jealous, envious or egotistical.
- Earn the right to be confident.
- Never expect favors.
- Do not make excuses or alibis.
- Never lose faith or patience.
- Courtesy and politeness are the marks of a real man or woman; and in return, we receive the good will and affection of others.

Wooden adds—"Success comes from knowing that you did your best to become the best that you are capable of becoming."

You shall love...God with all your heart...soul... strength, and...mind; and your neighbor as yourself. (Luke 10:27)

Guide me, Holy Wisdom, in being the best person I can be, for love of You, my neighbor and myself.

A Simple Wish

Everyone has a talent, like playing an instrument or drawing. Photojournalist Linda Solomon decided to use her camera skills to help those who are less fortunate.

All 7-year-old Daysha Sierra wanted was a bed to sleep in, something most people take for granted. But the girl slept on the floor of a Salvation Army shelter. When Solomon asked her to create a wish list with pictures, the young girl was only interested in something everyone should have, shelter.

Daysha, along with other children at the shelter, created her Christmas special wish list. Then, thanks to Solomon, the Salvation Army set up a fundraiser to provide the money needed to make these children's dreams come true.

Instead of taking gifts and opportunities for granted, let's use our talents to help those who need the simplest, yet the most important things.

Offer to God a sacrifice of thanksgiving. (Psalm 50:14)

Generous God, may my sacrifices help those who lack even the barest necessities of a human life.

The Hannukah Miracle

Hannukah is a wonderful celebration of faith and of God's miraculous intervention.

About 167 B.C., during the Syrian-Greek occupation of Israel, Jews were killed and Judaism prohibited. The Jerusalem Temple was looted and an altar to Zeus was raised. The priest Mattathias and his five sons led a revolt. He was killed, but his sons recaptured the temple and cleansed it. Zeus' altar was destroyed, and a new altar of incense was built. They set a Menorah or seven branched candelabrum before the altar.

But although the Menorah was supposed to be a perpetual light, there was oil for only one day. Rabbi Abraham J. Twerski says, they lit "the Menorah anyway, reasoning that it was best to do what was within their ability to do and to postpone worrying about the next day until such worry was appropriate."

Thanks to God, that one day's supply of olive oil burned for eight days.

> **On the twenty-fifth day of...Chislev, in the one hundred forty-eighth year, they...offered sacrifice... on the new altar of burnt offering. ...They celebrated the dedication of the altar.**
> **(1 Maccabees 4:52-53, 56)**

God, help us keep the Commandments to the best of our ability.

Stopping Holiday Anxieties

Things to do and to buy. People to visit and parties to attend. Oh the stress of the Christmas Season! But there are ways to get through the holidays with good cheer.

Map it out. Get out a pencil and paper, and write down what you need to do. Cross things off as you do them!

Decide what is most important. Prioritize the essentials, like spending time with family and friends, and do these first.

Delegate or delay. If there are things that aren't urgent, put them off until the new year. Enlist the help of others where you can.

Sometimes, just say, "No!" You can't go to every party or event and that's okay!

In all the rush, stay focused on the reason for the season—the birth of Jesus, God's love made manifest in our world.

Joseph...went to be registered with Mary, to whom he was engaged and who was expecting a child....She gave birth to her firstborn son and wrapped him in bands of cloth, and laid him in a manger. (Luke 2:4,5-6,7)

We celebrate Your great love for us, Father! In the birth of Your Son, we rejoice!

A Remarkable Recovery and Discovery

Jill Bolte Taylor lived through a rare form of stroke that shut down the left hemisphere of her brain. For months, she was unable to walk, talk, read, write or recall her life's events.

Eight grueling years of rehab enabled her to regain full brain function. But most remarkable is Taylor's newfound ability to achieve a state of peace, tranquility and well-being—a gift the stroke itself bestowed upon her.

In the years her brain was partially inoperative, Taylor found the absence of the left brain's "mental chatter" blissful. Today, she has mastered the ability to regain that state, "working" her brain selectively and quieting her left brain when stress mounts or when she needs to relax. "I can consciously choose to prevent the left side of my brain from dominating my life," she says.

Taylor's story is an example of seeing life's "glass half full." Extract the blessing inherent in all experiences, good and bad.

If we hope for what we do not see, we wait for it with patience. (Romans 8:25)

Grace us with optimism and gratitude, Father.

Mending Shattered Memories

As a child, Toni DePaoli treasured the Hummel Nativity set that had belonged to her grandmother and that had been passed on to her.

Years later, when her dad was diagnosed with liver cancer, he told her that he would send her the Nativity set. "They are yours," he told DePaoli. "That's what Grandma wanted."

But when the precious Hummel crèche arrived, it was shattered. Her grief nearly overwhelmed her. After her dad's death, she couldn't bring herself to open the box of broken memories.

One day, she came home to find the set on display in her living room, fully restored. It seems that her husband had found an artisan who restored the treasured statues.

DePaoli's grief had been transformed into gratitude and joy, thanks to a loving act of kindness. When was the last time you did something special for a loved one?

Clothe yourselves with compassion, kindness, humility, meekness, and patience. Bear with one another...forgive each other. ...Clothe yourselves with love. (Colossians 3:12-13,14)

Help me, God who wrote Your law of love in my heart, to show my love toward family.

A Father's Forgiveness

Tony Hicks grew up never knowing his father. His teenage mother knew little about parenting. His grandfather Ples Feliz tried his best, but Hicks still became a part of the California gang scene.

Fulfilling a gang initiation rite (rob the pizza delivery guy) Hicks shot and killed college student Tariq Khamisa. "It was as if a nuclear bomb had gone off in my heart," recalls the young man's father, Azim Khamisa when he learned of his son's death.

A devout Muslim, Khamisa used meditation to cope, releasing his anger and finding peace in his heart. He met with Hicks and his grandfather, forgiving them. And he started the Tariq Khamisa Foundation to stop youth violence.

Feliz and Khamisa travel the country and have personally reached 350,000 children with their message of nonviolence.

Tragic events can knock us to the ground. Standing up by God's grace, we can continue life's journey.

Filled with compassion; he ran and put his arms around him and kissed him. (Luke 15:20)

Merciful Savior, help me forgive others as You moment-by-moment forgive me.

Facing Up to Abuse

People who love you should not hurt you. That doesn't mean that we don't occasionally say a thoughtless word or commit an unkind act. No, we're talking about abuse—physical, sexual, verbal, emotional—that destroys the soul and often the body.

It can happen to people of any age or background. And victims need to accept the fact that the situation is not their fault and that the situation will not get better over time. They need to get help as quickly as possible.

It isn't easy for someone experiencing abuse to come to this realization, but when they do, help and protection are available. In addition to local resources the National Domestic Violence Hotline (1-800-799-SAFE) provides information and encouragement.

If you know an adult who is being abused, encourage them to get assistance and protection. If a child is being abused, you may need to call local authorities yourself. Trust God. Take action.

Do not fear, for I have redeemed you; I have called you by name, you are Mine. (Isaiah 43:1)

Grant us Your strength, Loving God. Help us find the resources we need to protect ourselves and others.

Patience Is More than a Virtue

Have you ever heard the prayer, "Give me patience, God—and give it to me now! It probably makes you smile because you know just how easy it is to lose patience over the littlest thing.

This is what St. Francis de Sales had to say about the subject: "Have patience with all things but first with yourself. Never confuse your mistakes with your value as a human being. You are a perfectly valuable, creative, worthwhile person simply because you exist. And no amount of triumphs or tribulations can ever change that. Unconditional self-acceptance is the core of a peaceful mind."

Try to be at peace with yourself and those around you—family members, friends, co-workers, neighbors and strangers—and to show patience for your own sake and theirs. And remember to be gentle and accepting of yourself as well.

You shall not take vengeance or bear a grudge against any of your people but you shall love your neighbor as yourself. (Leviticus 19:18)

Help me to accept myself and others for the imperfect, but growing individuals that we are, Gracious Father.

A Truly Interfaith Effort

In 1939, three nights before the German Army arrived in Auschwitz, Poland, a synagogue's sexton buried most of a Torah (the Five Books of Moses: Genesis, Exodus, Leviticus, Numbers, and Deuteronomy) in a metal box for safekeeping. Jews sneaked the remainder of the Torah into Auschwitz concentration camp!

Before they were put to death, these prisoners told a Catholic priest, who was a prisoner in Auschwitz because he was of Jewish birth, about the Torah.

Decades later Rabbi Menachem Youlus of the Save a Torah foundation and that aged Polish priest recovered the Torah. It was kept in the Ark of Manhattan's Central Synagogue until scribes could repair it and return it to Auschwitz.

This story is a reminder that hate is weak; respect, strong; that hate destroys, respect builds. Be strong, build a peaceful world, respect everyone without exception.

The genealogy of Jesus...the son of David, the son of Abraham....Jacob (was) the father of Joseph the husband of Mary, of whom Jesus was born, who is called the Messiah.
(Matthew 1:1,16)

God, remind Christians that Jesus lived and died a faithful Jew.

Santa's Little Helper

During the Christmas season people buy gifts for loved ones, but some also give presents to those in need.

Betty Frezon still had the beautiful Christmas stockings her mother made her as a child. Looking at them, she said, "I wish every kid could have a special stocking." So she decided to contribute her own hand-sewn stockings to the Rensselaer County (NY) Concerns-U, a store that takes donated toys and clothes and lets low income parents chose gifts for their children.

Frezon then got her quilting group involved. They traced, cut, sewed and donated over 500 stockings. Then parents at Concern-U chose toys and treats and put them into a handmade stocking for each child.

Let this holy season inspire you not only to give to your own family, but to families in need of some joy in difficult times.

See what almsgiving accomplishes. (Tobit 14:11)

What can I do, Jesus, to help others enjoy Your Birthday?

Chocolate as a Way of Life

Chocolate is a means to survival and independence for Ecuador's Quechua people. On a small island in the Napo River, Cesar and Magdalena Daua grow cacao. It's part of a new and increasingly successful cooperative that assures growers access to more lucrative markets, greater transportation options and fair-trade practices.

In the past, cacao farmers like the Dauas received a meager 20 cents a pound for intensely hard work. Today, volunteers like Judy Logback help cacao farmers improve their standard of living by earning an adequate profit. She teaches them enhanced growing techniques, more efficient transport of their crop to market and how to negotiate more favorable trading terms.

Choose socially responsible products when shopping. Look for products that promote fair-trade practices and livable wages for farmers and producers.

What gain have the workers from their toil? (Ecclesiastes 3:9)

Paraclete, inspire my support for the world's working poor.

Recapture the Joy!

The Christmas holidays are a time of worship, joy, celebrations, but sometimes of sadness and disappointment, too.

Maybe you feel pressured to spend time with difficult relatives. Or you can't get all the cleaning, shopping, gift wrapping and cooking done on time. Perhaps your loved ones are far away or deceased and you feel isolated, or sad.

How can you find the joy that is hidden in the celebration of Jesus' birth?

Start by acknowledging anger, grief or sadness and still be grateful for the blessings you do have. Remember that confession is a great way to start fresh during Advent. Make an effort to forgive others. Do something for someone else. And, especially, try to leave yesterday in the past.

Even though I walk through the darkest valley, I fear no evil; for You are with me. ...You prepare a table before me. (Psalm 23:4,5)

Good Shepherd, remember the sheep of your own fold, the lambs of your own flock who struggle to be joyful.

Building Peace from Within

Most of us think of ourselves as people of peace and good will. Yet how often we condemn others, judging them to be hate-filled or prejudiced or violent?

Even if we are basically decent people, surely we are far from perfect. But do we think about our faults and how we can improve ourselves—rather than pointing fingers at others?

Thomas Merton, the author and Trappist monk, wrote in *New Seeds of Contemplation:* "Instead of loving what you think is peace, love other people and love God above all. And instead of hating the people you think are warmakers, hate the appetites and the disorder in your own soul, which are the causes of war. If you love peace, then hate injustice, hate tyranny, hate greed—but hate these in yourself, not in another."

Let's love ourselves and each other as we try to grow joyfully and humbly in God's grace.

A harvest of righteousness is sown in peace for those who make peace. (James 3:18)

Heart of Christ, make my heart more like Yours.

Teens, Turkeys and Lots of Deliveries

Usually the students from Omaha's Catholic high schools are in heated competition, either for sports, drama or speech.

But each Christmas season they act as one, collecting turkeys and other foods to feed some 1,600 area families in need.

For the past 40 years, the student-run program, Operation Others, has helped teens tap into our God-centered call to love our neighbor. "It helps you refocus," says teen Justine Sacco.

Offers high school senior Jason Passarelli, "Delivering the food is probably the coolest thing of all. To see the smiles on people's faces is something you can't really describe."

In reaching out to lift up others, we renew God's love in our own hearts and lives.

Give, and it will be given to you. A good measure, pressed down, shaken together, running over, will be put into your lap; for the measure you give will be the measure you get back. (Luke 6:38)

Enable us to hear and answer those in need, Father.

Candyland Is Alive and Well

If your sweet tooth has been urging you to nibble more candy lately, you're not the only one.

When the economy started to slide in 2008, candy sales began to rise. According to an article in *The New York Times* many adults are lifting their spirits by indulging in simple, inexpensive, nostalgic candy.

Mary Janes, Gummy Bears, Bit-O-Honeys and more are thriving and so are their sellers and manufacturers. The same thing happened in the 1930's, when a number of still-popular items were introduced, including Snickers, Tootsie Pops and Three Musketeers.

Piper Gray, a young woman from Memphis seeking a job as a journalist in Manhattan, said, "Apples and oatmeal only go so far. It's so tempting to pick up an 88-cent pack of Skittles as a little pick-me-up. So I won't feel so deprived."

Nobody enjoys being deprived, but we need to carefully balance our needs with our wants.

Decide with equity for the meek. (Isaiah 11:4)

Redeemer, guide me in making the best decisions I can for myself and those who count on me.

Avoid Myths and Assumptions

"Even widely held medical beliefs require examination or re-examination. Both physicians and non-physicians sometimes believe things about our bodies that are just not true."

Those are the words of Dr. Aaron Carroll and Dr. Rachel Vreeman of the Indiana University School of Medicine who studied some popular beliefs related to health around the holidays and found them to be myths.

Sugar makes kids hyperactive. Twelve different studies found no basis for this idea.

Suicide increases over the holidays. Actually, they appear to be more common during warm, sunny days.

Poinsettias are toxic. Humans don't actually die or suffer serious poisoning, although they may be dangerous to pets.

Hangovers can be cured. No. There's no proof of any real cure.

We assume many ideas we hear or read are true. Stop. Get the facts. Then think things through.

The Spirit of truth...will guide you into all the truth. (John 16:13)

Bless me, Spirit of Knowledge, with Your gifts and help me share them with others.

When One Person C.A.R.E.S.

Angelo Cervasio's suicide note did not explain why he took his life. The Air Force veteran rarely drank, never used illegal drugs, and didn't seem depressed. At first his mother Virginia Cervasio blamed herself for anything she might have missed. Then, she formed C.A.R.E.S. (Community Awareness in Recognizing and Educating on Suicide).

Cervasio began visiting local service groups, foundations, and corporations. Everyone preferred avoiding the topic of suicide. But she persisted in telling her son's story and in explaining that in the United States someone commits suicide every sixteen minutes. C.A.R.E.S. also operates a suicide-prevention center offering counseling, referrals, and support groups staffed by volunteers with licensed therapists on call.

Whatever sorrow you may endure, allow yourself to be guided by God's mercy.

Comfort all who mourn...give them a garland instead of ashes, the oil of gladness instead of mourning. (Isaiah 61:2,3)

How can we bring hope to the hopeless, Blessed Trinity?

A Terrifically Tacky Tour

It's not unusual at Christmas time for people to visit houses with elaborate displays of lights and holiday decorations. In the Richmond, Virginia, area folks even have the "Tacky Light Tour."

But in *Guideposts,* Barbara Cole recounts how she and her co-workers had their own "Tacky Cubicle Tour." They used lights, tinsel, garlands, etc. to decorate their workspaces. To choose the winner each staff member votes with donations of cans, jars and boxes of non-perishable food. The cubicle with the most points wins. More importantly, the food goes to the Central Virginia Foodbank, 1,000 pounds worth in one year.

"When all the lights and tinsel are put away, what remains at the heart of the Christmas season is the spirit of giving," says Cole. "And that is truly sacred."

If you keep My commandments, you will abide in My love, just as I have kept My Father's commandments and abide in His love. (John 15:10)

Jesus, Son of God, Son of Mary, help me to give to others with joy and generosity, with mercy and merriment. Help me celebrate Your birth every day of my life.

Baked Inside Each Bite

Jennifer Steinhauer, the daughter of an interfaith marriage, is Jewish. Yet, she can never forget her grandmother's Christmas cookies.

Steinhauer fondly reminisces about the painstaking detail her grandmother devoted to hand making 15 to 20 unique varieties of delicate, delectable and decorated Christmas cookies.

From cheery wreaths to wafers dipped in colored sugar to charming gingerbread men, each dressed in ornate frosting, the cookies remain in Steinhauer's memory as firmly as her grandmother herself, who is now too infirm to bake cookies.

Says Steinhauer, "Though today I fashion my gingerbread into dreidels and menorahs, as I bake from her recipes I feel close to her arms, working the dough."

In whatever way we honor those we love we ensure that they and our love for them endures for today and tomorrow.

Rise before the aged, and defer to the old... I am the Lord. (Leviticus 19:32)

Thank You, Father God, for those whom You have sent to care for me. May I keep their memories alive.

Latte Lifesaver

Michael Gates Gill once earned $160,000 as an advertising executive. But at 53, he lost that job. A failed business and divorce followed, along with the diagnosis of a brain tumor.

One day, he found himself sitting in his local Starbucks, dressed in a business suit. The manager asked if he wanted a job. He took it.

Today, still working there, Gill lives a simple life. He's grateful his brain tumor hasn't grown and that he doesn't need surgery. He even wrote about his experience in a book called *How Starbucks Saved My Life: A Son of Privilege Learns to Live Like Everyone Else*.

"What you are doing is trying to help other people enjoy something," he explains about his work.

Life can change in an instant. Count on the resilience of your own spirit, the spark of God's life within you, to help you and those around you.

Will not God grant justice to His chosen ones who cry to Him day and night? Will He delay long in helping them? I tell you, He will quickly grant justice to them. (Luke 18:7-8)

Grant me Your strength, Master, to face life's challenges.

Where We Are, Where We Go

At the beginning of a new year, many people yearn to change their lives for the better. But to do that, we need to understand where we have been and where we are.

"Although God calls us all toward a more perfect life, we cannot personally achieve the state of perfection," writes Dr. Gerald May in *Addictions and Grace*. "We can and should do our very best to move in that direction, struggling with every resource we have, but we must also accept the reality of our incompleteness which is the empty side of our longing for God and for love. It is what draws us toward God and one another."

Our life's journey isn't measured in miles or hours, or even by the beat of our heart, but by the faith, hope and love we share. And our success? That comes from getting up just one more time than we fall.

Those who look into the perfect law, the law of liberty, and persevere...will be blessed in their doing. (James 1:25)

Generous Father, remind me that You love and long for me even more than I love and long for You.

Wrapping Up Feelings

Maggie loved Christmas. In the weeks before the holiday, she would decorate, shop for just the right gifts, plan visits, even host her own Christmas Eve open house.

Then knee replacement surgery, scheduled just six weeks before Christmas, ended all those traditional plans. What would she do? She had to at least give everyone gifts. Then it dawned on her. She would give her word—words, in fact.

In the weeks before her surgery, Maggie wrote messages of thanks and love to all her family and friends, describing the ways they had blessed her life. She framed the tributes, matched to her favorite photograph of each person.

No matter the time of year, the greatest gift we can receive—or give others—is love. It's the perfect fit for every heart.

**Love one another deeply from the heart.
(1 Peter 1:22)**

Lord, I give You praise for the blessing of family and friends.

The Gift of a Stranger

One December evening, Pat Allen found herself in a low place, a rough patch in her life and became saddened. The Christmas season could not cheer her up, since she felt that only bad things would continue to happen.

Passing a gift shop, she saw a plush white bear and decided to treat herself, hoping it would make her feel better. While on line, she began to cry and the man in front of her asked if she was OK. She told him what she had been going through and that the bear was to help cheer her up.

When it was time for the cashier to ring up his charges the man added the cost of the stuffed bear to his tab, saying to Pat Allen, "I just want you to know that good things do still happen."

We are never alone; it only takes one stranger to be kind to someone down on their luck, having a rough patch.

Be merciful, just as your Father is merciful. (Luke 6:36)

Thank You, Generous God, for the many people who have extended the hand of loving kindness to me in times of misery.

Celebrating a Blue Christmas

While Christmas is a time of joy for most Christians, some struggle at this time.

"There are so many people who are lonely or grieving loss or bad family histories," says Father Larry Rice, director of the Newman Center at Ohio State University. "For them, a holiday with all the expectations of merriment can be alienating."

So the Newman Center invites local people to a special "Blue Christmas" Eve Mass. Several hundred usually attend. While the Mass is traditional, the tone is low-key.

Father Rice adds that "The homily is directed more toward the core, theological meaning of the Incarnation, of God joining us in our struggles and our pain."

A number of participants remark that it's the first Christmas service where they have felt comfortable in years.

Reach out to those near you who are having a hard time.

The Lord has...sent me to bring good news to the oppressed, to bind up the brokenhearted. (Isaiah 61:1)

Merciful Savior, enable us to see how we can comfort those who are troubled.

Flowers of the Holy Night

Among the many decorations enjoyed at Christmas, is the poinsettia. Known for its bright red color, the plant was named for Joel Robert Poinsett, an amateur botanist and the first U. S. ambassador to Mexico.

But the Mexican name for the plant is Flores de Noche Buena or Flowers of the Holy Night. According to legend, a little girl longed to bring a gift to the Infant Jesus at Christmas, but she was so poor she had nothing. Her cousin told her that even a humble gift offered with love would be welcomed, so she gathered a bunch of roadside weeds. When she entered the church and laid the bouquet in front of the Nativity scene it burst into the beautiful flowers we've come to love.

Legend or not, it's true that God appreciates the simplest gift from the heart, if it's presented with love.

Wise men from the East...(followed) the star... until it stopped over the place where the Child was. ...They...paid Him homage. Then...they offered Him gifts of gold, frankincense, and myrrh. (Matthew 2:1,9,11)

Child of Bethlehem, let every gift of mine be one of love for You. And may I share that love with all Your children.

Post-Christmas Gifts

'Tis still the season to be jolly and generous. Continue to give to the folks in your neighborhood:

- Offer snow-shoveling services to an elderly neighbor.
- Help an immigrant learn English through your library or volunteer group.
- Donate your clean, but unused or unwanted clothes to churches, the Salvation Army, or other groups assisting the needy.
- Volunteer for a local park clean-up day.
- Send a book, DVD or video game to hospitalized children.
- Mentor an at-risk teen.
- Give blood.

These simple deeds can make a big difference in someone's world. Plan some acts of charity as the New Year begins.

Be rich in good works, generous. (1 Timothy 6:18)

Inspire us to deeds of charity and loving kindness, Holy Spirit.

Do You Need a Hug?

Hugs are the newest greeting in schools nationwide. Gone are simple "Hellos," high-fives, and handshakes. Hugs popularity has skyrocketed. Why a hug?

One student says it is comforting and much more exciting than a high-five. A teacher believes hugging is a "sign that children are inclined to nurture one another."

Yet others criticize this greeting. A parent complains that hugging no longer has any special significance. "It's superficial," according to one disapproving student. Some schools have gone so far as to ban hugging. One school principal says hugging is pointless.

Still, people will continue to use hugging as a way to express their feelings and maintain human contact. Whether it's a handshake, high-five or hug, greet someone with warmth and compassion.

Greet one another with a holy kiss. (1 Corinthians 16:20)

Jesus who expressed Your emotions honestly and sincerely, help us imitate Your emotional honesty.

Singing for Sanitation?

Mozambique knows him as one of southern Africa's most celebrated musicians. Feliciano Dos Santos sings haunting, beautiful songs to which most of his fans relate.

But recently Dos Santos changed his tune. When performing for impoverished villagers, he sings of healthy habits, the importance of boiling water before drinking and ways to keep water sources sanitary.

Dos Santos is educating the poor on ways to curb the spread of diseases caused by poor sanitation and unfiltered drinking water. As a toddler, he contracted polio, which is often spread through contaminated water and food. Today, a charity he founded, Estamos, or *We Are,* promotes clean water and safe sanitation for communities in Southern Africa.

There are countless ways you can help make this world a better place. Using your unique talents and abilities, find a way to serve others in a way only you can!

There was a disciple whose name was Tabitha, which in Greek is Dorcas. She was devoted to good works and acts of charity. (Acts 9:36)

Emmanuel, Remind me that every effort to serve others is worthwhile.

Driving Permit

Do you have a car? Imagine you couldn't drive it in your neighborhood. Imagine you had to keep it in an expensive parking lot at some distance.

Residents of Vauban, Germany have done just that. The town does not permit cars on roads, except on the main street. Seventy-percent of the town's population does not own cars. Those who do paid $40,000 for a parking spot at the edge of town. The community, opened in 2006, is designed with stores, hospitals, and schools within easy walking and biking distances from homes.

The town seeks to lower pollution levels, while providing empty streets as a safer play area for children.

Nations worldwide are helping their congested cities by planning more walkways and encouraging public transportation. Carpool to work and school. Walk more. The Earth will appreciate it.

God the Lord, speaks. ...The world and all that is in it is mine. (Psalm 50:1,12)

Thank You, Creator, for the loveliness of Earth and all its creatures.

Helping Others From Behind Bars

Jaymie Powers, a 43-year old mother of three grown children who is in prison for second-degree murder, has found a new purpose in life.

Powers is one of many women at New York's Bedford Hills Correctional Facility who participate in a program called Puppies Behind Bars, in which inmates help train service dogs to assist disabled people.

"One of things prison usually means is being useless," says another Bedford Hills inmate. "The program gives me a sense I can be useful to people on the outside," she adds.

Powers works with dogs like Devon, a Labrador Retriever who listens to Powers' commands and is learning to flip light switches, shut doors or take off socks.

Another inmate says, "We give people who receive these dogs their freedom, something that we've lost."

How can you serve others, too?

The Lord sets the prisoners free. (Psalm 146:7)

Inspire us to serve others, Blessed Trinity.

Time to Resolve

This is the time of year when we make resolutions. Kathleen Choi, in the *Hawaii Catholic Herald,* offers these suggestions to benefit not only you but others:

- Don't volunteer for anything you're not really going to do.
- Never badmouth other races or religions; or people of the opposite gender or political party.
- Admit when you're wrong
- Pay attention. "You only pass this way once."
- If you say you'll pray for someone, do so.
- Smile.
- Choose carefully what you read, watch or listen to.
- Be careful about teasing.
- Sit still, be quiet and just breathe, daily.

Live your life gently, respectfully, mindfully, lovingly, purposefully, prayerfully.

If you wish to enter into life, keep the commandments. (Matthew 19:17)

Author of life, help me live the life You've given me as well as I can.

Also Available

Have you enjoyed volume 44 of *Three Minutes a Day*? These other Christopher offerings may interest you:

- **News Notes** – published 10 times a year on a variety of topics of current interest. Single copies are free; quantity orders available.

- **Ecos Cristóforos** – Spanish translations of select News Notes. Issued 6 times a year. Single copies are free; quantity orders available.

- **Wall Calendar and Monthly Planner** – The Calendar offers an inspirational message for each day. The Monthly Planner with its trim, practical design also offers a monthly inspirational message.

- **DVDs** – Christopher videos range from wholesome entertainment to serious discussions of family life and current social and spiritual issues.

For more information on The Christophers or to receive **News Notes, Ecos Cristóforos** or a catalogue:

The Christophers
5 Hanover Square
11th Floor
New York, NY 10004
Phone: 212-759-4050 / 888-298-4050
E-mail: mail@christophers.org
Website: www.christophers.org

The Christophers is a non-profit media organization founded in 1945. We share the message of personal responsibility and service to God and humanity with people of all faiths and no particular faith. Gifts are welcome and tax-deductible. Our legal title for wills is The Christophers, Inc.